POSITIONING TOURISM DESTINATIONS

Allen Z. Reich

Northern Arizona University

SAGAMORE PUBLISHING

Champaign, Illinois

www.sagamorepub.com

Interior Layout: Michelle R. Dressen
Cover Design: Julie L. Denzer

ISBN: 1-57167-261-3
Library of Congress Card Catalog Number: 99-61358

Printed in the United States of America.

■ Aim & Scope of Series

ADVANCES IN TOURISM APPLICATIONS provides a new forum for organizing and presenting emerging theory and management practices in five broadly defined areas of tourism management: (1) destination marketing, (2) destination management, (3) environment, (4) policy, and (5) statistics and theory. This new series of monographs attempts to fill an important gap between textbooks and journal articles, representing a comprehensive discussion of the most current theories and/or practices by leading scholars and industry professionals. Each volume identifies and discusses the most current theories and/or practices relevant to a specific topic, provides concrete examples and explanations of the importance of these theories/practices to the tourism industry, and provides extensive bibliographic resources.

As editors of the series, we want to encourage and facilitate the creativity of researchers and managers in tourism. Specifically, we invite readers to contribute by submitting manuscripts and/or case studies which describe innovative applications in the tourism industry. We welcome your ideas and suggestions for future topics and look forward to joining you on this journey of building knowledge for the 21st century.

. . . .

Dr. Daniel R. Fesenmaier
Dept. of Leisure Studies
University of Illinois at
Urbana-Champaign
Champaign, IL USA

Dr. Joseph T. O'Leary
Dept. of Forestry &
Natural Resources
Purdue University
W. Lafayette, IN USA

Dr. Musaffer S. Uysal
Dept. of Hospitality and
Tourism Management
Virginia Polytechnic Institute
Blacksburg, VA USA

Other titles currently available in the
Advances in Tourism Applications Series

Contents

CHAPTER FOUR
The Positioning Process

■ Preface

WHETHER AN individual business or a geographic location, every tourism destination has one or more primary markets and several secondary markets from which it attracts the majority of its visitors. The ability to attract these markets segments is based on the destination's *market position*—its image in the minds of customers relative to competitors. The existing and desired positions of a tourist destination are critical and complicated issues in strategic market management. With literally thousands of potential variables to analyze, the determination of the most suitable strategic path is a daunting one. The decision to remain with current strategies or to change them, the degree of change, and the acceptability of new strategies carries with it the success or failure of the destination.

Travel and marketing have been two of the most important concepts in the history of mankind. Because of their increasingly rapid pace of change, bedrock principles of these disciplines are concurrently undergoing constant analysis and modification (Mansfeld, 1992). Historically, marketing theory initially focused almost exclusively on selling. The first attempt at a more scientific approach to marketing came from the Taylor Society (named after Frederick Taylor, the father of scientific management) in the 1920s, and it was not until 1957 that the first text was published that proposed a marketing planning orientation (Alderson, 1957).

From a theoretical standpoint, marketing is amazingly still in a vigorous growth stage. Each year brings groundbreaking research that challenges previous assumptions. Additionally, the quality of marketing and strategic research has vastly improved over the past several decades. However, because of the human need to explain and the natural evolution of free markets, there will always be a need to improve upon existing concepts and theories. Wind and Robertson (1983), both prominent strategy researchers, proposed that researchers regularly assess the value of components of marketing strategy and their implications to the structure and work of the marketing function.

This monograph focuses on the application of the concept of positioning as applied to tourism. The objectives are to:

1. Review positioning's place in the tourism and hospitality industry, and business in general

2. Analyze the primary construct of positioning—image and its impact on behavior
3. Research past important work on the positioning process
4. Develop a more effective and understandable positioning process that is applicable to the tourism industry

A new, theoretically based conceptual framework for determining a destination's ideal market position will be presented, one that will lend logic and rationality to an often subjective process. Concepts to be covered include:

- Linear positioning—a quantification of a destination's and its competitors' existing market positions.
- Market/profit position matrix—a prescriptive model that can be used to assess the firm's current market and profit positions, plus help identify the firm's ideal market and profit positions. [In this usage market position represents the totality of a firm's efforts at establishing its image in the marketplace (e.g., marketing, operations, human resources, finance, etc.).]
- Strategic aggression—a typology that can be used to identify the logic behind strategic change and the potential outcomes of that change.
- Additional quantitative and qualitative means of determining the most logical solution to the positioning question.

1
Positioning in the Tourism Marketplace

EVERY TOURISM destination has one or more primary markets and several secondary markets from which it attracts the majority of its guests (Bonn & Brand, 1995; Perdue, 1996). The ability to attract these markets segments is based, to a great extent, on the destination's position[1] (read, *market position*) (Calantone & Mazanec, 1991; Barich & Kotler, 1991; Herbig & Milewicz, 1993; Jeffrey & Xie, 1995). Positioning is a critical issue because it establishes the foundation of existing and future customers' image of the destination and, subsequently, the basis for their behavior. It is essentially the consumer's reference point when determining whether to purchase from one supplier or another (Puto, 1987). Consequently, managers of destinations must develop the analytical skills and processes necessary for them to understand and effectively monitor and modify their destination's current position (Adler, 1968).

Effective positioning is based on management's knowledge and abilities relative to those of competing destinations. H. A. Simon (1993) addressed this when he stressed the need for an effective matching of key strategic abilities (anticipating the future, generating viable options, and effective implementation) with opportunities in the environment. Essentially, offer customers a superior product at a reasonable price and they will be less likely to visit competitors.

As important as a firm's position is, relatively little research and only minor industry attention have been paid to the topic. In marketing texts it rarely garners more than a few pages. Most marketing plans give it only superficial attention. Why does this occur? Have researchers and strategists chosen not to dwell any longer on planning efforts than absolutely necessary? Do they not fully understand the importance of positioning? Have planners been satisfied that the firm's mission statement sufficiently described its desired position? Whatever the reason, it is time for strategists to consider the importance of positioning to the firm's planning and implementational efforts.

The task of positioning for tourism destinations has been addressed by several authors, primarily through its key construct of image (Fridgen, 1987; Gartner, 1989; Gartner & Hunt, 1987; Reilly, 1990; Reilly & Millikin, 1994). These articles have provided a wonderful base of knowledge that can assist destination managers in learning about their area's relevant attributes. However, there is more to positioning than simply image. This is a subject that deserves more attention and updated methods. The purpose of this monograph is to research existing positioning research and positioning processes, then to provide a theoretically based process that can help managers maximize the position of their destination.

In this monograph, *managers of destinations,* generally marketing managers, are assumed to be working for any organization in one region (city, county, state, country, etc.) that must attract consumers from other points of origin. Typical organizations in which these managers work include tourism bureaus, chambers of commerce, governmental travel and tourism agencies, marketing coops, economic development organizations, and hotels and restaurants that cater to the traveling public (Hill & Shaw, 1995; Palmer & Bejou, 1995).

Position Defined

Position, a noun, is generally defined as *the image in the minds of customers relative to competitors* (Assael, 1985; Bateson, 1989; Boyd & Walker, 1990; Cravens, 1991; Kotler, 1991; Lewis, Chambers, & Chacko; 1995; Lovelock, 1991; Morrison, 1989; Peter & Donnelly, 1991; Powers, 1990; Quelch, Dolan, & Kosnik, 1993; Ring, Newton, Borden, & Farris, 1989; Urban & Star, 1991). The hypothetical position for a destination's leisure segment could include: "The Bahamas is a safe tropical destination that is reasonably inexpensive; with excellent shopping, sight-seeing, boating, snorkeling, scuba, and gaming facilities; a pleasant year-round temperature; is convenient to central and eastern U.S. cities, and is the favorite Atlantic Ocean destination of U.S. residents."

> *In the planning process, positioning can be looked upon as the junction point between the destination's corporate- and business-level strategies and its functional-level strategies.*

Positioning, a verb, is the systematic process of analysis and decision making that guides managers in locating the most suitable and profitable place in the minds of customers relative to competitors. It is based on achieving compatibility between the destination's attributes and the demands of one or more market segments, and the subsequent targeted promotion of that position/image (Reilly, 1990). In the planning process, positioning can be looked upon as the junction point between the destination's corporate- and business-level strategies and its functional-level strategies (see *Positioning's Place in the Planning Process,* in this chapter). Corporate- and business-level strategies emphasize the future overall strategic focus of the destination. Positioning will entail describing how the firm wants to be viewed by customers after it has implemented corporate- and business-level strategies. Functional-level strategies are designed to help the destination achieve its desired position. (Positioning can be viewed as the last component of business-level strategies or placed between business- and functional-level strategies.)

Repositioning

When major changes in the destination's current position are required to remain competitive, the destination will attempt to *reposition* itself in the market (Quelch et al., 1993). Managers who let their market position slide, whether through neglect or poor strategic decisions, are gambling with their destination's future (Hurley, 1990). Keeping a destination at its present position is far simpler than being forced into a repositioning situation. Making incremental improvements to the destination's position on an annual basis carries only minimal risks and consistent levels of effort and expenses. Repositioning places the entire future of the destination in jeopardy. While generally not as risky and expensive as developing a new destination, changing the perception of an existing destination's target markets can cost millions, with no guarantee of positive results.

Categories of Positions

A destination's position can be discussed from two primary perspectives, its *strategized position*[2] (also referred to as the *subjective position*)—an explicit or implicit positioning statement—and the *objective position*—overall opinion of the target market. The strategized position is important from the perspective of the firm's past accuracy in predicting and influencing customer demand and opinion and its effectiveness in implementational efforts. In other words, how successfully did the firm's managers create and implement their position, and how well was it received by customers? Were there changes in how the destination is viewed? Were these changes compatible with the destination's strategized position? The objective position is important because it represents the image target customers have of the destination relative to competing destinations. When the term *position* is used, it is important to know its context. In most cases, its usage refers to the destination's objective position.

Differences between the two positions represent a gap that will have likely consequences for the destination. This gap could be based on the implementation of a poorly designed strategy or through having poorly implemented a well-conceived strategy. Most successful destinations will have their strategized and objective positions in relative agreement. For example, if the strategized position, or management's view, was that one's hotel is a first-rate midscale hotel with clean rooms, fast check-in and check-out, and friendly service, the objective position should reflect this. If not, there may be a problem (a gap or non-alignment). If management thought that its menu selection and quality were just what the customer wanted, but in reality they were not, sales volume would suffer and future opportunities might be missed. In addition to helping the firm locate its ideal position, consumer research can help managers help expose ineffective and poorly implemented strategized positions.

Sometimes the problem of non-alignment of strategized and objective positions is not serious. In one hotel, management did not consider the implications of being near a city recreation center to be important; however, its guests considered exercise to be important. In this case there was not a major problem, but simply a missed opportunity. It is possible that a certain number of potential guests would have selected the hotel if they had known about the nearby recreation facilities. This hotel's management was not maximizing its potential within its market. If exercise is what guests value, then it should be included in positioning decisions, acted upon, and promoted.

POSITION AS A FACTOR OF PRODUCT OFFERING, PROMOTIONAL, AND PUBLIC IMAGE

In the hospitality industry, the majority of a destination's position is based on its *product offering* (rather than promotional or public image). This occurs because much of the public's perception of the industry's products is often based on either first-hand experience (an organic image formation agent) or the experience of a friend or acquaintance (unsolicited or solicited organic image formation agents). In fact, for American consumers, the market penetration of the vast majority of hotel and restaurant concepts is near 100 percent. For example, most upscale travelers have stayed at Hilton, Sheraton, Marriott, Hyatt, and Doubletree hotels (and likewise for upscale restaurants). The percentage would certainly be lower for many geographic destinations; however, product offerings based on organic agent perceptions still dominate hospitality positioning. In contrast, the position of many manufacturing firms (e.g., durable products) is based more on promotional efforts. The reason for this is that most consumers of refrigerators, for example, have very little knowledge of brands other than their own. They generally do purchase a variety of refrigerators over a several-year period, and they do not visit friends to examine their refrigerators and ask questions about them. Promotional and public image do play an important part in hospitality marketing strategies, but their primary influence is on increasing awareness among potential consumers and on increasing the loyalty of existing consumers.

The *promotional image* concerns the overall message that has been communicated through personal (individuals) and nonpersonal channels (mass media). As with the customers' perception of the destination's position, there may be a vast difference between what customers think of the destination's promotional efforts and what management thinks. Often, destinations with excellent or satisfactory sales or visitations assume that no changes are necessary in promotional efforts and the image or message they project. In some cases this will be true, yet a problem arises when the destination's internal efforts are at standards that keep existing customers returning on a regular basis, but external promotional efforts are lacking. Subpar promotions may not be adequate to replace regular customers that are siphoned off by competitors or who no longer travel to the destination's trade area. This should be viewed as a positional weakness that must be evaluated and corrected (Deighton, Henderson, & Neslin, 1994). External communications should set the destination apart from competitors; offer benefits that target market demands, including those that are most critical to the purchase decision; communicate a mental of image of what the business stands for; and deliver on what the message promises (Lewis, 1990).

The destination's *public image* is derived from individuals' exposure to any information about the firm. Sources include publicity from charitable and other community-oriented efforts, its reputation as a good place to work, the reputation of its management, word-of-mouth advertising, and the business's external appearance (Schmitt, Simonson, & Marcus, 1995). This image should be considered not only among its target customers, but also in the local communities in which it operates and in the broader public. The importance of public image increases when buying power is concentrated and represents a major risk to the decision maker. For example, a corporate travel planner, in determining the geographic destination and hotel for a 2,000-room-night national conference, will be making a career-defining decision.

POSITIONING'S PURPOSE

Positioning serves decision makers in four critical areas (Calantone & Manzanec, 1991; DiMingo, 1988; Haahti, 1986; Lovelock, 1991; Wind & Robertson, 1983). It (1) exposes the relationship between customer satisfaction and the performance of the destination and competing locations; (2) helps to identify new market opportunities; (3) matches product and service offerings with that desired by the target market (selection of appropriate strategies); and (4) communicates to the target market through personal and nonpersonal communication channels that the destination's offering is unique and preferable to competitors' offerings. The basic goal or purpose of positioning is to achieve top-of-mind awareness (TOMA), also referred to as being first on the customer's product ladder. This is the conscious or subconscious list of destinations that are reviewed each time a purchase is considered (Ankomah, Crompton, & Baker, 1996). [The concepts of TOMA and customer's product ladder are closely related to choice set analysis, where the goal is first to be in the decision set (best alternatives set), and subsequently, in the choice set (see Schiffman & Kanuk, 1991; Spiggle & Sewall, 1987).] A tourist destination's place on its customers' product ladder is

> The basic goal or purpose of positioning is to achieve top-of-mind awareness (TOMA), also referred to as being first on the customer's product ladder. This is the conscious or subconscious list of destinations that are reviewed each time a purchase is considered.

based on (1) the business's and geographic destination's strategists' selection of positioning strategies, (2) the functional strategies chosen to articulate the positioning strategy, (3) the success with which the functional strategies are implemented and communicated, and (4) the degree to which competitors' positioning and supportive functional strategies have met the demands of the target customers.

The ultimate objective in the positioning process is to maximize a firm's abilities in its market through the selection of an appropriate image and supportive strategies (Wind & Robertson, 1983). Some of these strategies should concentrate on the development of strategic or distinct competencies (Porter, 1991), ideally resulting in a *sustainable competitive advantage* (SCA) (Aaker, 1988). An SCA is a characteristic of the business that is attractive to target customers, represents an advantage over competitors, and ideally can be protected or sustained for approximately one year or more.

Practical Importance

Conceptually, it would be difficult to conceive of a more meaningful business concept. To be positively thought of by one's target customers, relative to competitors, is an attribute that the vast majority of businesses aspire to (Herbig & Milewicz, 1993). Some destinations are blessed by the nature of their product and environment (e.g., first mover advantage, product-class loyalty—a budget restaurant chain; the image of the product's class—upscale business; or its place in the product's life cycle—introduction or growth) with a highly positive position (Schnedler, 1996). Others have worked diligently to acquire an attractive position. Whichever the case, the maintenance of at least a satisfactory position is the ultimate responsibility of all people associated with the destination or business (Barich & Kotler, 1991).

Cognitively, we know that managers make decisions that they presume will allow their destination to either hold on to or improve its current standing in the market. These decisions are often broadly categorized as strategies, tactics (policies and action plans), and routine supervisory decisions. Each of these decisions communicates to guests what the destination or business has to offer, and to employees, their part in the destination's overall effort. The term *position* may not be used, inferred, or understood by management or employees, but the employees know by what managers consider to be important that a certain standard of performance (strategized position) is being pursued. Likewise, customers have their own personalized image of the destination which they use to consciously and subconsciously position the business among alternative offerings. The problem with understanding this situation is that because of a void in research literature, little is known about (1) whether these decisions are based upon an explicit positioning process, and (2) the possible algorithms of specific positioning processes.

Practitioners are generally thought to use the concept of positioning (Mazanec, 1995), but there has been little formal research to support this supposition. It is difficult to imagine that academicians have been advocating its use without knowing if and how it is being used. Is there a reason for this vacuum? Perhaps positioning is such a vague concept that its meaning, importance, and appropriate application are interpreted differently by academic researchers and practitioners, and by members within each group. Is it possible that because of positioning's multi-variable composition it is only an implicit evaluation en route to setting various strategies (e.g., price, quality, convenience, and so forth)? Or is the preparation of a formal, written, positioning statement the norm? Do any firms consider their overall hierarchical position in comparison to competitors (how a business ranks compared to its chief rivals)? Could it be that the term is primarily reserved for the analysis of advertising (brand positioning) or other business decisions, such as achieving differentiation (Haahti, 1986)?

One could ask, "How could academic researchers have different interpretations of a basic marketing concept?" One study found a similar problem with the misunderstanding and subsequent misuse of the commonly used marketing terms *market segmentation* and *product differentiation*. In this study they found that textbook authors were divided into essentially two camps: those who believed that product differentiation and market segmentation were synonymous, and those who viewed product differentiation as a means of implementing a market segmentation strategy.

Academic Arena

According to researchers, *positioning* is the third step in a process following (1) segmentation and (2) market targeting (Haahti, 1986; Lamb, Hair, & McDaniel, 1994; McCarthy & Perreault, 1993; Ring et al., 1989; Urban & Star, 1991). A destination's position, generally expressed in the form of a positioning statement, should include and integrate relevant information from the customer analysis and other pertinent portions of the firm's situational analysis. Once the positioning decision is made, it becomes a critical standard for all existing, modified, and newly adopted business- and functional-level strategies and tactics (Boyd & Walker, 1990). Because of this sequence, the positioning decision forms much of the basis for a destination's image and subsequently the degree of its financial success (Curry, 1985).

Compared to its apparent importance, positioning has received only nominal coverage in the literature. Of the 15 or more marketing textbooks that have currently been reviewed for this study, only Cravens (1991), Lewis, Chambers, and Chacko (1995), and Urban and Star (1991) set aside either a chapter or a major portion of one for the discussion of positioning. A review of over a decade of the *Journal of Marketing* uncovered only one article focused primarily on positioning and with positioning in its title (Shostack, 1987). Though a few hospitality researchers such as Dev, Morgan, and Shoemaker (1995) and Shaw (1992) have written on the topic, few except for Lewis (1981, 1982, 1985, 1990) have produced a significant body of positioning research.

Why is the coverage of positioning focused in textbooks rather than journals? Is it because of its general nature and the difficulty in specifying its constructs and variables? Could it be that it is covered, but another term, such as *image*, serves as a surrogate for the concept of positioning? These questions and others must be answered if both researchers and practitioners are to maximize their efforts on this important concept.

POSITIONING'S PLACE IN THE PLANNING PROCESS

The initial source of information for the positioning process is the situational analysis (see Reich, 1997b, for guidance on preparing a situational analysis for a hospitality organization). Here, market managers must determine their destination's strengths and weaknesses relative to the demands of the selected target markets. Marketers then must determine the opportunities and threats in their destination's environment. The SWOT analysis (the strengths and weaknesses of the business and the opportunities and threats of the environment) is a summary of all data and information from the situational analysis. Of primary concern in the environmental analysis is the segmentation of potential markets and the selection of the most viable markets (the targeted traveler). These processes are referred to respectively as market segmentation and market targeting. The Strategic Analysis Questioning Sequence is a list of questions that helps management determine the variables from the SWOT analysis that should be considered or utilized in strategic decisions and the remainder of the planning processes (Reich, 1997b).

Next, managers from various functional departments along with top management must determine the destination's *corporate- and business-level* strategies (defined below). Marketing managers must decide how they want customers within those markets to view its product offering relative to competing offers—its desired position (embodied/made explicit in a positioning statement). Subsequently, marketing managers and those of other functional departments will need to develop functional-level strategies supportive of corporate- and business-level strategic decisions and the destination's chosen position. Positioning is normally either associated with business-level strategic decisions or prepared as a separate component between business-level and functional-level strategies. The following is a review of the three levels of strategy.

1. *Corporate-level decisions.* These decisions are normally associated with multi-business corporations, but to varying extents, must also be made by single-business corporations (see the bottom left portion of Figure 1.1). The types of decisions made at the corporate-level often concern:

   a. The corporation's public and internal image,
   b. The degree of social responsibility desired,
   c. Major resource allocations, for example, basic strategy decisions of whether to:
      - Grow—invest in the business with hopes of future profits.
      - Hold or milk—keep the business at its present operating and financial level while investing profits in other business units.
      - Harvest—skim off most profits while reinvesting only enough to keep the business solvent.
      - Divest—sell the business.
   d. Decisions on what businesses the corporation should be involved in,

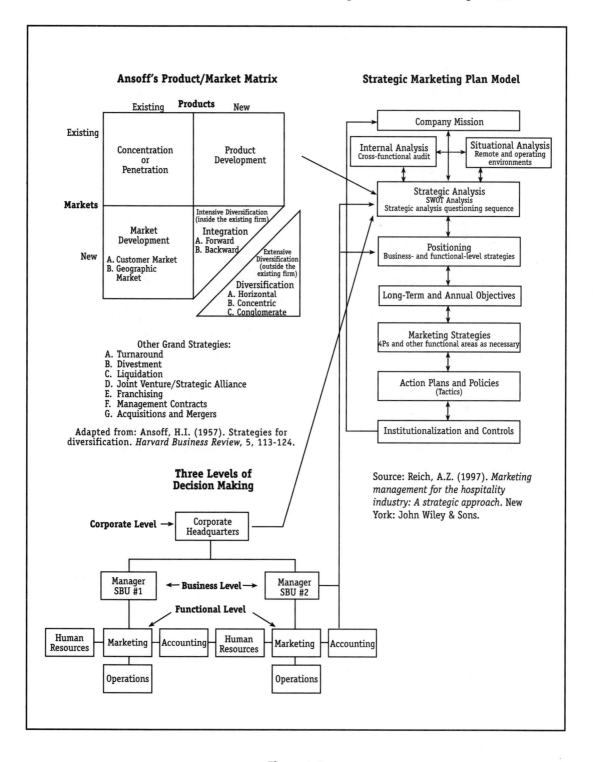

Figure 1.1:
Corporate-level decisions

e. Selection of managers/presidents for business units,

f. Setting of strategic parameters and key objectives for business units: The corporate level will prepare the corporate mission statement and assist in writing the mission statement for the individual businesses.

2. *Business-level strategies.* Business-level strategies are concerned with how the business will compete in its particular industry. These decisions will focus on the firm's product mix, customer and geographic markets to serve, how it can exploit its distinct competencies (major strengths), and the achievement of one or more sustainable competitive advantages (Olsen, Tse, & West, 1992). Business- and corporate-level strategies are the long-term portion of the strategic plan.

3. *Functional-level decisions.* These are made by the managers and employees of various functional departments (e.g., marketing, finance/accounting, human resources, and operations). Functional-level decisions are primarily concerned with creating specific strategies and tactics that support the objectives and strategies set by the corporate- and business-level managers. For example, if a business-level strategy were to increase the number of association visitations, a functional-level strategy might be to utilize brochures, and the accompanying tactic could be to send them to associations where members have household incomes over $65,000.

Argument over Positioning's Location in the Planning Process

Though strategists generally agree that positioning is a strategic rather than a functional or operational issue, they disagree over which part of the organization should be responsible for it. To help emphasize the delineation between strategic management and other types of managerial decisions, Schendel (a professor of strategic management)(1985) in a conference proceeding (Thomas & Gardner, 1985), differentiated between strategic marketing and marketing at the operations level. Marketing is a functional area that coordinates with, and is no less or more important than, other functional areas. Strategic aspects of marketing, and other functional areas, include efforts in the development of strategy, primarily in attaining a competitive advantage, and helping to achieve strategic goals. Schendel specifies that goals for marketing should be viewed primarily as top-down rather than bottom-up. His reasoning was that "strategic goals, while not necessarily formulated on a strictly top-down basis, in fact must act that way, if the hierarchy of strategic goals is to be consistent among vertical organization levels and horizontally across functional areas" (p. 54). Strategic goals for marketing come from business-level strategy decisions that are in turn developed based on corporate-level decisions. It is appropriate for operating goals for marketing and other functional areas to originate internally because the focus is on efficiency. He goes on to say (p. 54):

> *It would be confusing for the finance function to be working toward different growth goals than those set for the marketing function, or for manufacturing to be working toward one capacity level while marketing works toward a different one. Hence, only where the marketing function is as-*

signed a strategic goal, as for example in the extension of geographic scope, would there exist the need for strategic action on the part of marketing.

Schendel states that issues, such as *market position,* competitor analyses, and the firm's position within the product life cycle, are devised by strategic management at the business level. He does, however, give marketing credit for being an important source of environmental information. Marketing is essentially concerned with the tactics of the marketing mix; strategic marketing occurs only as support is necessary for strategic management. To confirm his opinion on the supporting role of marketing, he adds the following:

> *There is in some marketing literature the notion that marketing is the starting point of the strategic planning process. In this view, nothing can really happen until marketing, working from the mandate of the marketing concept, initiates the strategy. While such a notion may have appeal to some, it oversimplifies what is a very complex undertaking, which may or may not proceed from a bottom-up view as implied by the idea of marketing as the center of the planning universe. . . . Anyone experienced with strategic planning work realizes there is no reason why 'strategic marketing' has to be the lead function in strategic planning. In fact, an argument can be made against such a starting point.*

Schendel (also see Galbraith & Schendel, 1983) says that strategy begins the planning process, that both corporate- and business-level strategy is the domain of strategic management, that marketing is concerned with functional strategy and goals (and therefore environmental factors that affect functional strategy and goals), and that marketing is a support system of strategy. He then uses a quote of Kotler to support his statements about the role of marketing in setting strategy. Kotler's statement, however, contradicts many of Schendel's assertions.

> *Management is the entrepreneurial agent that interprets market needs and translates them into satisfactory products and services. To do this, management goes through a strategic planning process and a marketing process. The strategic planning process describes the steps taken at the corporate and divisional levels to develop long-run strategies for survival and growth. This provides the context for the market process, which describes the steps taken at the product and market levels to develop viable market positions and programs. (Kotler, p. 9, and Schendel, p. 59, cited in Thomas & Gardner, 1985)*

While Kotler does say that management is the responsible agent for strategic decision making, he offers several contradictions—contradictions that should have been evident to Schendel. The following are some of the areas where Kotler's quote is inconsistent with Schendel's statements:

1. Specifying "entrepreneurial agent," Kotler is referring to the concept that the business begins with the customer. Covin (1991) says that among the reasons that entrepreneurial firms frequently outperform conservative firms are an increased propensity toward risk; usually smaller, less bureaucratic organizations (this statement is directly counter to Schendel's assertion of the need for a "consistent . . . hierarchy" of decision making); and the need of strategies that help differentiate themselves from larger competitors. This not only allows, but requires the entrepreneurial firm to take a more proactive stance when it comes to taking advantage of potential opportunities. Conservative firms, on the other hand, tend to be risk-averse, non-innovative, and reactive.

Therefore, an "entrepreneurial agent that interprets market needs and translates them into satisfactory products and services" does not work in a "consistent. . . hierarchy," or look upon strategy as beginning at the top. Strategic planning is not devised by ivory tower philosophers, but by entrepreneurs willing to innovate and take risks (Drucker, 1985). Entrepreneurs see opportunities in the environment that others have missed, in addition to maximizing existing sources of revenue.

2. Kotler states that "management goes through a strategic planning process and a marketing process." Kotler views these processes as parallel as seen in steps 1 and 2 of Figure 1.2 (Kotler, 1991, p. 63). Strategically, marketing information is the primary source of information used by strategic planners (this could be a strategic-planning department or simply the top manager of a business) to make decisions. Marketing and other applicable functional plans are then prepared and implemented. The results are evaluated and analyzed in light of new marketing information.

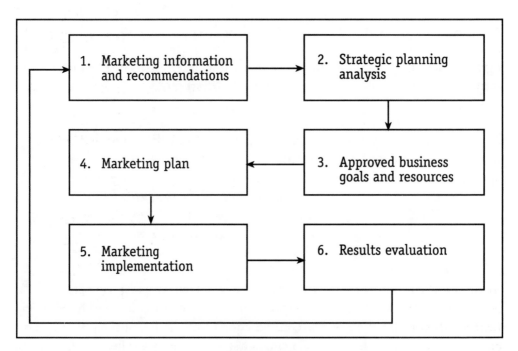

Figure 1.2:
Parallel planning: Marketing and strategic planning

3. Kotler's last statement, "This provides the context for the market process, which describes the steps taken at the product and market levels to develop viable market positions and programs," does not support Schendel's statements. Here Kotler says that marketing develops:

A. *Product and market strategies.* These are the bases for all other strategies. Once the product and market selections have been made, and related strategies and objectives established, other functional areas can then support strategies and objectives.

B. *Viable market positions.* Market positions can be interpreted in several ways—brands, products, relative to competitors, and in some circumstances position in the product or industry life cycles. Since Kotler (1991) looks upon positioning as "designing the company's offer so that it occupies a distinct and valued place in the target customers' minds" (p. 302), product positioning would be the likely context and interpretation of "market positions."

Who Is Responsible for Positioning? Strategic Management vs. Strategic Marketing

From the literature, the place for ultimate responsibility for the positioning decision depends on the perspective of the researcher. Apparently top management, under the title strategic management, is attempting to work its way down the decision hierarchy, while marketing, under the title strategic marketing, is trying to work its way up (see Figure 1.3). Notably, two of the top strategic management textbooks did not mention the term positioning (Thompson & Strickland, 1993), while every marketing textbook reviewed for this research discussed it as an important element of marketing strategy. The definition itself—image in the minds of customers relative to competitors—points to a marketing orientation. This is what marketers do. Marketers determine position, while top management determines whether the position is appropriate for the business's situation.

> The definition itself—image in the minds of customers relative to competitors—points to a marketing orientation. This is what marketers do. Marketers determine position, while top management determines whether the position is appropriate for the business's situation.

KEY CONCEPTS IN POSITIONING

As a matter of record, the management of every firm sets functional strategies (Keller, 1993). Without these, no firm could exist. But as the planning process is traced back to its inception, there is less evidence, and therefore minimal accountability, of the strategic process and positioning decisions that influenced

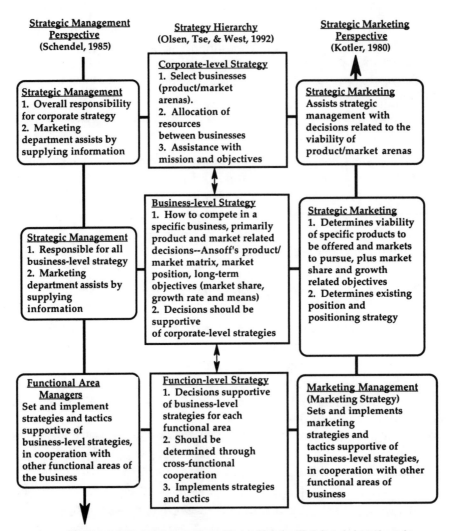

Sources: Schendel, D. E. (1985). Strategic Management and Strategic Marketing: What's Strategic about either one? In H. Thomas and D. Gardner (Eds.) Strategic marketing and management (pp. 41-63). New York: John Wiley. Olsen, M. D., Tse, E. C., & West, J. J. (1992). Strategic Management in the hospitality industry. New York: John Wiley.

Figure 1.3:
Positioning: Who is responsible?
Strategic management vs. strategic marketing

functional strategies. Having an organized process that requires objective analysis and produces accountable decisions can improve a destination's positioning efforts.

Linear Positioning

Marketing managers (also strategic planners) are well aware of the importance of the position of their geographic location (Bramwell & Rawding, 1996). Contemporary corporate, unit, and geographic destination marketing plans generally include survey data (e.g., positioning maps and statistical tables) that provide management with a reasonably accurate picture of the destination's position (Yuan & Yuan, 1996). While this form of multi-attribute analysis is valuable in determining the destination's future position, it ignores an important issue. It does not offer the competitive panorama necessary to help managers determine the optimum level of overall change required for the coming planning period. This occurs because the traditional positioning process often neglects to pinpoint the hierarchical or linear position relative to competitors. This linear position (market position or relative-market position) does not refer to the multi-attribute analysis that is normally located on various positioning maps (also referred to as perceptual maps and multi-dimensional scaling), but on a composite position that presents the linear relationship between the destination, its primary competitors, and its external environment.

Since the linear position is a relative ranking based on consumers' images of the destination, it must be recognized that these images are based on more than just marketing efforts. Each functional unit within a destination will have an impact on its overall relative position. For example, it is the employees of the destination that carry out applicable production and service functions. Whether specific functions are controlled by a department within a business, such as human resources, operations, reservations, financial, and so forth, or by an association with a vested interest in improving the quality of guests' experiences, the totality of the position will represent the efforts of each functional area.

Market/Profit Position Matrix

No matter how attractive a destination's linear position, if it is not producing a suitable level of profit, its appropriateness must be questioned. Most destinations and businesses can achieve high linear-position rankings by lowering their prices, increasing promotions, or making significant improvements in facilities. Each of these strategies, however, brings with it the possibility of decreased profits (this could be any measure of profits, such as return of sales, investment, or assets managed). Therefore, as management deals with the decision to change its market position, it will concurrently need to assess the change's impact on profitability.

Strategic Aggression

Once the linear position (market position) and profit position have been determined, management can then view the firm from the broad perspective of not only customer satisfaction, but also how well the firm is positioned for the future. Management's awareness of its linear position leads to a glaringly obvious question. "What should we do about it?" or better, "How aggressive (strategic aggression) should we be in attempting to improve our current position?" An average position may be the best management can hope for if the cost of improving the position is greater than the potential return. Additionally, in situations where visitor traffic is satisfactory, the firm's financial ratios are in line, and the environment is relatively stable, then perhaps this average position is acceptable to management and stakeholders. If, however, the destination's position is far behind what it is capable of, then a change in its current degree of strategic aggression should be considered. Internal abilities and environmental dynamics will dictate the need for change (Ireland, Hitt, Bettis, & De Porras, 1987; Tse, 1988). The risk that management and stakeholders are willing to accept will determine the degree. The decision to modify the firm's overall position and by what degree is often left unanswered because of modern management's tendency to focus on details and functional priorities, rather than the big picture.

The application of the preceding concepts requires managers to carefully analyze their current position relative to competitive circumstances, then commit to a certain level of strategic aggression. These concepts are also excellent tools for historically analyzing a firm's past successes and failures. Holiday Inn, a leader in the midscale hotel segment from the 1950s through the 1970s, saw its position decline gradually during the 1980s. The firm's main problem was that, while it may or may not have recognized that its position was changing, it failed to adapt. Rather than making incremental changes during this time, management waited to act until its image had plummeted. Subsequently, their attempts at improving their position have not been aggressive enough for the market to reward them with a better position.

PLAN OF MONOGRAPH

The monograph will proceed with a review of image as a construct in tourism and the measurement of the attitude of image (Chapter 2). These two topics form much of the basis for positioning decisions. Next will be a review of positioning research and positioning processes suggested by various authors (Chapter 3). Finally, a detailed positioning process will be offered (Chapter 4). This process is based on current and seminal research and a conceptually new method for determining the most appropriate position and means of attaining it.

ENDNOTES

[1] In marketing terminology, the single-word term *position* refers to an organization's *position in its market* or its *market position*. The term *position* is generally associated with the marketing function. A destination (or any organization) can also have positions related to any key aspect or function. For example, it could have a have a *profit position* (its profit relative to other competing destinations) and a position related to human resources (image in the mind of actual and potential employees, plus guests' image of working conditions).

[2] Because the strategized position is a determined by management, rather than by the destination's guests, it can also be referred to as the subjective position.

■ 2
Positioning and Image

THE CONSTRUCT of *image* forms the foundation for the study of positioning. It is a highly intangible construct that can be defined in many ways and operationalized by a countless number of variables. For example, while image is derived from both intrinsic and extrinsic elements, its basis is the perception or opinions that individuals have regarding those elements. Reilly & Millikin (1994) found that image (for tourism) has suffered from "definitional, conceptual, and methodological differences" (p. 1) that have detrimentally affected its role in research. However, in spite of these challenges, its measurement has been studied and attempted by several reputable researchers (Bramwell & Rawding, 1996; Echtner & Ritchie, 1993; Fridgen, 1987; Gartner and Hunt, 1987; Gartner, 1989; Reilly, 1990).

Image Defined

The following definitions of image are representative of those found in various sources. *Webster's New World Dictionary* defines image as "4. (a) a mental picture of something; conception; idea; impression (b) the concept of a person, product, institution, etc. held by the general public, often one deliberately created or modified by publicity, advertising, propaganda, etc." (Guralnik, 1986). Dichter (1964, p. 75) describes image as "not individual traits or qualities, but the total impression an entity makes on the minds of others." Tuan (1975, p. 208, cited in Fridgen, 1987, p. 102) offered, "Image can be thought of as a mental representation of an object, person, place, or event which is not physically before the observer." Kotler (1991, p. 570) notes that image is "the set of beliefs, ideas, and impressions that a person holds of an object." Echtner and Ritchie (1991) suggested that "destination image should be composed of perceptions of individual attributes (such as climate, accommodation facilities, friendliness of the people) as well as more holistic impressions (mental pictures or imagery) of the place" (p. 3). Embacher & Buttle (1989) utilized the World Tourism Organization's definition: "Image is . . . comprised of the ideas of conceptions held individually or collectively of the destinations under investigation. Image may comprise both cognitive and evaluative components" (p. 3).

While each of the above definitions has variations, their common characteristic is a *mental impression of an object*. Tuan increases the specificity of the definition by adding that image concerns impressions about something that is not physically before the observer. This addition is to help differentiate the less tangible construct—image—from the more tangible—percept (perception)—"we see what is before us" (cited in Fridgen, 1987, p. 102). For research purposes, this avoids the confusion of distinguishing between image during an experience—a perception—and image before or after an experience (away from the evaluated object). Therefore, according to Tuan, image is in our minds, physically removed from the object of concern, while perception is based on our current (real-time) experience with the object.

Customer-Based Brand Equity

A broader extension of image, brand equity, is defined as "the incremental discounted future cash flows that would result from a product having its brand name in comparison with the proceeds that would accrue if the same product did not have that brand name" (Simon & Sullivan, 1990, cited in Keller, 1993, p. 1). A more concise definition was offered by Keller, "the differential effect of brand knowledge on consumer response to the marketing of the brand" (p. 2), in other words, the value of the image of the entity (geographic destination, hotel, restaurant, etc.). Brand equity is composed of two constructs, brand awareness—recall and recognition—and brand image—associations of increasing abstraction and scope (attributes, benefits, and attitudes) that customers hold in their memory which are linked to the brand (see Figure 2.1). Brand associations are important because these are part of the *associative network memory model,* a system of nodes and links (Anderson, 1983; Wyer & Srull, 1989, cited in Keller, 1993). Information is stored in the nodes, and the nodes are connected by means of linkages. As either new information is entered or existing information is accessed, the nodes are activated. Consequently, the manner in which a consumer has linked various pieces of information about a business (favorability, strength, and uniqueness) influences the consumer's perception of the business. In a related experiment that supports this concept, Alba and Chattopadhyay (1986) found that increasing the salience of one brand can limit the recall of competing brands. This was found

> **B**rand equity is composed of two constructs, brand awareness—recall and recognition—and brand image—associations of increasing abstraction and scope (attributes, benefits, and attitudes) that customers hold in their memory which are linked to the brand.

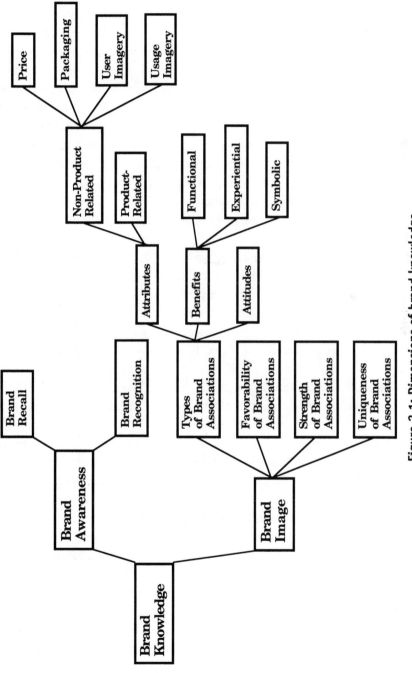

Figure 2.1: Dimensions of brand knowledge

Source: Keller, K.L. (1993). Conceptualizing, measuring, and managing customer-based brand equity. *Journal of Marketing, 57* (1), p. 7.

to be true, even in instances when the competing brands would normally be contained within the consumer's normal evoked set (known options).

The Image Construct

The destination's image, an attitude, is composed of three hierarchically ordered components: *cognitive*, images of the destination based on beliefs derived from all sources of information; *affect* (feelings), one's motivations for travel; and *conative*,[1] behavior or surrogates for behavior, such as intentions and preference (Gartner, 1993). The hierarchical relationship is that details (beliefs) about the destination are first developed in the cognitive stage. Here the details are evaluated for their positive, negative, or neutral impact on the individual. These beliefs are sometimes referred to as the *content*, or *rational* portion of a person's attitude (i.e., their image) toward an object. Since beliefs are perceptions about an object or action that may or may not be a predisposition to action, it is possible that beliefs alone would suffice as an attitude measurement. For example, "I believe that Country A is preferable to alternatives and the cost of transportation and lodging are reasonable, therefore that is where I will go."

The affective component concerns how strongly the individual feels about the particular belief—its personal relevance as a motivator. Depending on the purposes of the research, this feeling can be directed toward the object or toward the overall feeling that the object will lead to a certain behavior. An affective feeling toward an object might include: "I feel the price of the vacation is too high" (fair, too low, or other categories). An example of an affective feeling toward the behavior might include: "The price is too high, so I will not go there for my vacation." If the purpose of the research was to learn more about the beliefs people hold regarding a destination, the attitude toward the object may be more valuable. If, on the other hand, the purpose is to find out how the feeling impacts behavior, then attitude toward the action may be more appropriate. The question of the research option that is most beneficial is debatable. Even leading attitude researchers such as Fishbein and Rosenberg have different beliefs about which is best. Ultimately, each research option will yield actionable results. (This topic and the overall attitude structure will be discussed in greater detail later in this chapter.)

The conative stage is the behavioral result of either the cognitive stage alone ("the destination is peaceful and relaxing"), or both the cognitive and affective stages ("I need a relaxing break from work"). If the cognitive elements toward one destination are generally more positive than alternative destinations' and their affective components are similarly positive, then a decision of some type may be made. This decision could include placing the destination in a continuum of choice alternatives, including preference, intention, and choice. The consumer's choice set—reasonable alternatives—denotes a level of brand preference. The decision set—best alternatives—denotes brand preference or intention. That is, "I prefer these alternatives to others," or, "I intend to visit one of these destinations." The decision may also become the actual choice. Until the trip is undertaken, actual choice would generally indicate intention; once on the trip has begun, the choice has been made.

Image Agents

Gunn (1972) divided the development of an individual's cognitive image into induced and organic images.[2] Induced images are a function of the direct efforts of the geographic location, such as advertising in newspapers, television, and magazines, and indirect communications, such as publicity. Organic image includes information derived from personal visitations, friends, and acquaintances. Gartner (1993) further divided these two categories into various image formation agents:

- *Overt Induced I*: Direct attempts by the destination to influence image through traditional forms of advertising (mass media, such as print, television, radio, and the Internet). Indirect attempts at Overt Induced I could be pursued by sending brochures, videotapes, or other promotional materials to travel agents.

- *Overt Induced II*: This category includes information that has either been requested or sent without being requested from various travel intermediaries (travel agents, tour operators, travel wholesalers, and so forth). This category of information is often termed destination-specific travel literature (DSTL) (Mansfeld, 1992).

- *Covert Induced I*: This is the use of a celebrity to help communicate a message. It could be through a mass medium or by personal appearances. The effectiveness of this image agent is directly tied to the credibility and trustworthiness of the celebrity. Although this is not as strong as a third-party endorsement (an unbiased opinion), it can improve the chances of a promotional message having a positive impact on the destinations' image.

- *Covert Induced II*: In this image agent category, travel writers or organizations that have the ability to promote the destination receive some type of motivation to include the destination in their media sources. This is generally accomplished with a familiarization tour, where a travel writer or television program, in exchange for a free trip, will promote the destination. Though this may appear to consumers to be a third-party endorsement, it is simply a less costly and, generally, less effective means of advertising. The limited effectiveness is based on the restricted coverage of the media involved. While there are some travel magazines and travel shows (television programs) with moderate market penetration, most have rather small audiences.

- *Autonomous*: These image formation agents are not provided incentives to prepare and publicize information about the destination. This category is similar to publicity, with the exception that with publicity, there may be some form of covert contact. Since there is complete autonomy, the information reported should be unbiased. There is, however, the chance that a certain destination may not receive fair treatment because it is simply associated with an event that it has no control over. For example, if a news program discusses the fact that tourists were killed in one country, it may have an impact on tourism in nearby destinations.

- *Unsolicited Organic*: These agents provide unsolicited information about a destination. They are true third-party endorsers, who have either direct or indirect information about the destination. Since the majority of these agents are friends or acquaintances, their credibility is often higher than that of other image agents.

• *Solicited Organic*: These agents are quite similar to unsolicited organic agents, with the exception that the consumer has requested information about the destination. It differs from Overt Induced II in that the information provider does not have a vested interest in the outcome.

• *Organic*: This category includes personal visitations by the consumer. No other image formation agent can compare with personal contact. This is why the best and least expensive form of promotion is to provide existing guests with an exceptional experience. Not only are they more likely to return, but they will naturally tell their friends about their wonderful experience.

THE UNDERSTANDING AND MEASUREMENT OF ATTITUDE

The concept of attitude (image is an attitude) has been plagued with such ambiguity that two researchers, Doob (1947) and Blumer (1955) (both cited in Rokeach, 1968) recommended that its use as a scientific construct be discarded. Rather than abandoning attitude, Rokeach recommended "giving it a more precise conceptual and operational meaning" (p. 111). He defined attitude as "a relatively enduring organization of beliefs around an object or situation predisposing one to respond in some preferential manner" (p. 112). Rokeach's use of the word *preferential* in his definition is somewhat perplexing. He did not qualify it in any manner, so the reader is left to assume that he was referring to a positive attitude, rather than a neutral or negative attitude. Kerlinger (1980) uses the term *selective,* instead of *preferential.* Utilizing this definition in the context of positioning, the following could be said: "The image of a destination is a relatively enduring organization of beliefs predisposing one to respond in some consistent manner."

The following are properties of attitude offered by seminal attitude researchers:

• Beliefs are cognitions about the acceptance of something as true/real or false, good or bad. They are the basic unit of people's cognitive structure (Scott & Lamont, 1973).

• Beliefs can be measured by the intensity (strength or confidence) with which they are held and their centrality (Rokeach, 1968). The greater the intensity, the greater the likelihood that the belief will result in attitude change or behavior. Centrality denotes the salience or importance of the belief. Rokeach defined salience as the degree of connectedness of the belief with other beliefs (pp. 163-165). The implications being that the more connected a belief, the more important or salient that belief is to the individual.

• Attitudes are simply interrelated beliefs. That is, they are composed of two or more beliefs (Rokeach, 1968) (e.g., belief[1], "I believe that diet is associated with health"; belief[2], "I believe that exercise is associated with health"). This individual's attitude toward health might be composed of two or more beliefs (e.g., Attitude[1] = $b^1 + b^2$—if people eat the right foods and exercise, they will be healthier).

• Values are general beliefs concerning what is good or bad, desirable or not desirable, that are shared by individuals in societies. They are not directed toward any specific element, but used to assess a broad range of objects and situations (Scott & Lamont, 1973).

• Attitudes, and the beliefs they are based on, are enduring (Rokeach, 1968). That is, they provide psychological stability, allowing individuals to consistently respond to similar situations. For attitudes to be enduring they must be consistent in test-retest situations.

• Attitudes express an individual's cognitive criteria of acceptance (positive attitude), rejection (negative attitude), or noncommitment/neutrality towards some object (Sherif and Nevergall, 1965). "Being *against* something implies being *for* something else, and vice versa" (p. 19). In other words, an individual cannot have simultaneous pro and con attitudes on the same specific issue (e.g., someone cannot be both for and against the eating of animals on the grounds that it represents cruelty). An individual could have differing attitudes on different issues, but not on the same specific issue. Also, the importance of positions within an individual's personal schema can vary, as well as the degree of acceptance or objection to the positions of others (Sherif et al., 1965).

• Attitudes have an emotional component that influences an individual's motivation toward a social object (Sherif et al., 1965).

• Both the cognitive and affective components of attitudes are acquired (Rokeach, 1968). An individual will rank a destination's image based on his or her culture, social, and intellectual experiences (interaction in his or her environment).

• Since attitudes (and their cognitive and affective components) are predispostions to action, their activation may result in *behavior* (Rokeach, 1968; Rosenberg, 1956) (see Figure 2.2). Sherif et al. (1965) supported this when they wrote that when events do or do not agree with one's attitude, the behavior that results is highly predictable. Behavior (action) in this instance is a human social behavior based on the "rational and systematic" (Ajzen and Fishbein, 1980, p. 5) use of available information, rather than on unconscious motives. That is, in normal dealings with others, humans have a choice of how and whether to act.

Behavior is partitioned because not all attitudes will lead to action (Peter & Olson, 1990). For example, a person may have a positive attitude about a certain country's environmental efforts and a predisposition to support environmentally friendly destinations; however, because they do not like other aspects of the coun-

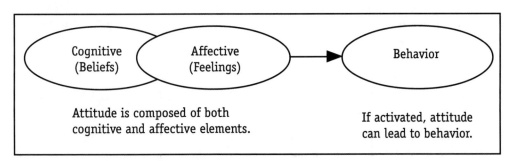

Figure 2.2: Attitude/behavior model

A s consumers are confronted with any situation, the totality of their attitudes, both cognitive and affective, will be summoned to determine whether action is desirable or necessary.

try, there is no predisposition toward action (visiting this country). This attitude/behavior situation would be representative of position 8 in the Attitude and Behavior Analysis Matrix (see Figure 2.3)—Positive Cognitive and Affect, Neutral Conative/Behavior. In other words, as consumers are confronted with any situation, the totality of their attitudes, both cognitive and affective, will be summoned to determine whether action is desirable or necessary.

Ajzen and Fishbein (1980) take a similar view of the relationship between the attitude components and behavior. In their *theory of reasoned action*, they do not refer to the attitude toward a certain phenomenon, but to the attitude toward the behavior and the social pressures (subjective norms) that may influence the behavior. For example, in some situations,

		Conative/Behavior		
		Negative	Neutral	Positive
Affect and Cognitive	Negative	**1** Dislikes firm's brand and purchases competing brand.	**2** Dislikes firm's brand, but does not purchase any brand of the product.	**3** Dislikes firm's brand, but still purchases it.
	Neutral	**4** Unaware or has no feeling about the firm's brand, and purchases a competing brand.	**5** Unaware or has no feeling about the firm's brand, and does not purchase any brand of the product.	**6** Aware of the firm's brand, has no strong feelings about it, but still purchases it.
	Positive	**7** Likes the firm's brand, but purchases a competing firm's brand.	**8** Likes the firm's brand, but does not purchase any brand of the product.	**9** Likes the firm's brand, and purchases it.

Figure 2.3: Attitude and behavior analysis matrix

Adapted from: Peter, J. P., & Olson, J. C. (1990). *Consumer behavior and marketing strategy* (2nd ed.). Homewood, Illinois: Irwin, p. 28.

such as special occasions or circumstances, an individual's attitude toward an object may have little impact on behavior. Some people may dislike salad but eat it because it is good for their health. Therefore, attitude toward the phenomenon could be measured, but have little influence on behavior. In a content analysis article, Wicker (1969) found the relationship between attitude and behavior to be relatively weak. Variables other than attitude that could potentially influence behavior include "conflicting attitudes; competing motives; verbal, intellectual, and social abilities; individual differences, such as personality characteristics; normative prescriptions of proper behavior; alternative behaviors available; and expected or actual consequences of the behavior" (Ajzen & Fishbein, 1980, p. 25). The concept of attitude toward behavior and normative prescriptions of proper behavior (subjective norms) are presented in Figure 2.4.

Attitude and Social Reinforcement

In an attempt to better define attitude, Kerlinger (1980) combined and modified the research of Allport (1935), Krech and Crutchfield (1948), and Rokeach (1960). He wrote that "attitudes are enduring and organized structures of social beliefs that predispose individuals to think, feel, perceive, and behave selectively toward referents or 'cognitive objects' of attitudes" (p. 5). In this definition, *think* and *feel* refer respectively to cognition and affect. *Perceive,* or perception, influences the individual's motivation to act/behave. *Behave* is used instead of Krech and Crutchfield's less direct *motivation. Referents* are the elements/objects to which the attitude of interest is directed, such as one's religion, political affiliation, family, government, and so forth (Sherif, et al., 1965). Kerlinger uses the term *critierial referents* to refer to attitudes that are shared by like individuals. Finally, this definition implies the concept of *social reinforcement*—attitudes that are supported by people important to the individual will exhibit greater centrality than those that are not similarly supported.

Beliefs

Since attitudes are composed of two or more beliefs, beliefs are the foundation upon which attitudes are based. Beliefs are often difficult to uncover. For various psycho-social or unconscious reasons, people may not be able to accurately articulate beliefs (Rokeach, 1968). A belief is often a statement preceded by, "I believe that . . ." (p. 113). It is therefore left up to the researcher to *infer* beliefs based on what the subject says or does (Sherif et al., 1965).

Beliefs can be utilized in three different contexts: *descriptive* (I believe that if I go outside without an umbrella when it is raining, I will get wet); *evaluative* (I believe that hamburgers are good); and *prescriptive* (I believe that people should obey speed limits).

In his seminal book, *Beliefs, Attitudes, and Values*, Rokeach (1968) began his research with three assumptions: (1) "Not all beliefs are equally important to the individual; beliefs vary along a central-peripheral dimension" (p. 3). Importance, in this context, refers to the degree of connectedness. The more connected a belief is

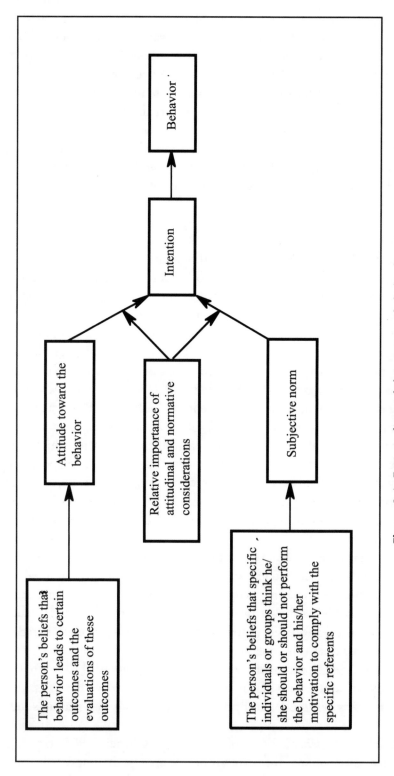

Figure 2.4: Factors determining a person's behavior

Source: Ajzen, I., & Fishbein, M. (1980). *Understanding attitudes and predicting social behavior.* Englewood Cliffs, New Jersey: Prentice Hall, p. 8.

with other beliefs, the more its centrality and the greater its impact on an individual's belief system/other beliefs. That is, beliefs regarding one's existence (existential) are more connected than nonexistential beliefs; shared beliefs are more connected than unshared beliefs; and arbitrary or judgmental beliefs, such as taste, are less well connected. (2) "The more central a belief, the more it will resist change." (3) "The more central the belief changed, the more widespread the repercussions in the rest of the belief system" (p. 3).

Rokeach's Belief Typology

Rokeach described beliefs in five groups lying on a continuum between centrality and peripheral dimensions:

- *Type A: Primitive Beliefs, 100 Percent Consensus*
  Those learned by direct contact and that are supported by one's reference groups.
- *Type B: Primitive Beliefs, Zero Consensus*
  Belief in God or phobias are strongly held beliefs that, though not necessarily supported by reference groups, may be highly central.
- *Type C: Authority Beliefs*
  At the point in which a child begins to be exposed to beliefs that contradict his or her primitive beliefs (e.g., religion, national, or ethnic pride, and foods that are acceptable to eat), nonprimitive beliefs begin to be formed. That is, there are other views and one's own views may not be widely held.
- *Type D: Derived Beliefs*
  As an individual is exposed to differing opinions from various reference groups (i.e., parents, friends, teachers), beliefs may be amenable to change based on other internally held beliefs.
- *Type E: Inconsequential Beliefs*
  These beliefs are generally expressed as personal taste or perceptions that may differ from experience to experience and will have relatively lower levels of centrality than previous beliefs.

Kerlinger's Belief Typology

Kerlinger (1980) developed an abbreviated and conceptually different belief structure. This typology is highly compatible with each of Rokeach's beliefs, except authority beliefs. Since authority beliefs are minor significant modifications of primitive beliefs, they can take the form of any other category of beliefs (Rokeach's or Kerlinger's). Kerlinger's typology consists of:

- *Knowledge Beliefs*
  Observations that an individual concludes to be true, but when analyzed, may or may not be true. For example, information in a brochure lauds a destination's courteous inhabitants. A customer could see this and believe that the destination's people are very nice, when in fact, the majority are quite rude. Since this belief may or may not be supported by factual evidence, it is a knowledge belief. Prejudice or negative stereotypes are based on these beliefs. Knowledge beliefs can usually be

empirically tested or proven to be either true or false. These are similar to Rokeach's primitive beliefs, 100% consensus.

- *Faith Beliefs*

These beliefs are more expressive than knowledge beliefs. They can generally be preceded by the phrase, "I believe in _____." For example, it would be difficult to prove or to empirically test the following statements: "I believe in minimizing governmental influence in business." "I believe that the president of our company is better than her predecessor." Kerlinger feels that faith beliefs are potentially more influential in human behavior than are knowledge beliefs. These are similar to Rokeach's primitive beliefs, zero consensus.

- *Opinion Beliefs*

If someone says that he "thinks" something is true, he is also recognizing the possibility that it may not be true. If someone says, "I think that Costa Rica is the most socially responsible South American country," he realizes that this may not be a recognized fact. These are similar to Rokeach's derived and inconsequential beliefs.

Belief and Attitude Development

An individual's attitudes can vary not only based on her beliefs, but also based on differences in *experience* and *involvement* (Sherif et al., 1965). These factors are important to attitude formation, since an individual with little experience will have minimally substantiated beliefs regarding a particular topic, and therefore will be more likely to be noncommittal or neutral. Once more experience has been gained; the negative or positive attitudes may surface. The influence of involvement would grow out of the individual's experiences and the centrality and salience of feelings they elicit. Because of its impact on survey reliability, this would be an important issue in belief or attitude measurement.

Resolving Belief Conflicts and Cognitive Consistency

While there are many theories related to how an individual resolves belief conflicts two of the most relevant to consumer behavior are Festinger's (1957) *cognitive dissonance* and Abelson's (1964) *belief dilemmas*. Festinger (1957) in his theory of cognitive dissonance,[3] attempted to describe changes in cognitive structure that result from inconsistencies between beliefs (and attitudes) and behavior. Any specific behavior will be based on a variety of beliefs. As these beliefs are questioned (i.e., "Was my experience satisfactory?") and either confirmed or disconfirmed ("Yes, it was" or "No, it was not"), beliefs will either be strengthened or weakened in some manner. Because dissonance deals with inconsistencies, it can occur after a positive or negative experience (Abelson & Rosenberg, 1964). After a positive experience (positive discomfirmation), the consumer may question the utility of alternatives (i.e., "Though my burger at McDonald's was good, if I had eaten at Wendy's, it would have probably tasted better"). Here, beliefs are less likely to be changed because the customer was satisfied with the experience and few inconsistencies between his or her expectations and firm performance were noted. However, after the negative experience, or discomfirmation (i.e., "The burger at McDonald's was not very good"), inconsistencies cause a greater level of dissonance ("I should have eaten at Wendy's"), and therefore a greater level of change in cognitive/belief structures.

Belief dilemmas[4] refer to the intrapersonal conflict an individual may have in deciding whether or not to act—internal cognitive and affective processes (Abelson, 1964). Abelson's typology of belief resolutions is more comprehensive than Festinger's theory of cognitive dissonance. As the individual considers taking any specific action toward an object, he will utilize these internal processes to reconcile the simultaneous positive and negative aspects of the object. Modes of resolution include:

• *Denial*

The value of the cognitive elements or relationships causing the imbalance are attacked. Once weakened, the new relationship can be used to justify new attitude or actions. For example, a consumer who values safety is confronted with the dilemma of choosing between Country A that offers a wonderful vacation experience, but whose image of being a safe destination is average, and Country B that offers an average vacation experience, but has an excellent record of safety. The dilemma is that, because of the two options, they are out of balance. If the consumer attacks his own beliefs about the importance of safety and goes to Country A, denial is being used to resolve the dilemma.

• *Bolstering*

The strengthening of the imbalance by including other cognitive elements in the belief relationship. If the same consumer in the denial example justifies restaurant B by adding other supportive beliefs, bolstering is being used. For example, cognitively, the consumer could think that the food quality is average, but add other beliefs that justify selection B. "The selection is good," "The service is better," "The location is more convenient," and so forth. Bolstering is very similar to cognitive dissonance.

In both denial and bolstering, the original cognitive elements are retained. Either the strength of a belief is weakened (denial) or additional beliefs are added to strengthen the original cognitive structure (bolstering).

• *Differentiation*

Here, one or more of the original cognitive elements are either eliminated and replaced by other beliefs or split into both positive and negative beliefs. For example, the high cost of a trip to Destination A (a negative belief) is divided into (1) cost of transportation (a negative belief) and (2) cost of lodging and food (a new positive aspect). The consumer has then resolved the dilemma through differentiating the negative cognitive belief. Differentiation can occur through internal content, as in the above example; social context, a division of the consumer's beliefs and that of society's; and divisions between current beliefs toward the object and beliefs of its ideal condition or potential future condition.

• *Transcendence*

Rather than replacing or dividing beliefs as in differentiation, transcendence combines existing cognitive elements, then adds a related and supportive element. A consumer could combine the beliefs about restaurant B into single hierarchically ordered belief (excellent SR/average food), then add a third belief (such as, "It's the right thing to do," "It feels good to help my community," "I'm a better person for doing this") to correct the original imbalance.

- *Conflict Resolution and Persuasion*

An individual's attempts at resolving conflicts (cognitive consistency) will be based on conflicting forces in the individual, by differences in cognitive ability (the ability to reason) (McGuire, 1964), and by the discrepancy between the individual's attitude toward a referent and that of opposing views (Sherif et al., 1965). The goal of the individual will be to maintain cognitive consistency. Related to persuasion, the goals of the marketer are to first create a conflict or imbalance in beliefs about the product or action being promoted, conflicts that are logical and understood, and subsequently to change consumers' beliefs/opinions to some measurable degree (e.g., likelihood of purchase or increase in preference). If the marketer has convinced the consumer that his product is different in positive ways, then an imbalance has occurred, the conflict is logical (the product is better), and the consumer's attitude has been changed.

Attitude's Place in Consumer Behavior and Marketing

Before consumer attitude toward any particular phenomena can be measured, the consumer must first be aware of the existence of the phenomena and, second, have beliefs about it (Rokeach, 1968). This relationship is partially explained by the hierarchy of effects model which shows the successive stages a consumer will normally progress through before a purchase is made (Dunn & Barban, 1978; Lamb, Hair, & McDaniel, 1994; Sirgy, 1997) (see Figure 2.5).

- *Unaware*

At some point all consumers are unaware of certain product options.
- *Aware*

They learn of various options through personal and nonpersonal (media) communication channels.
  - *Marketer's Task.* Promote awareness in potentially viable consumer markets.

- *Beliefs/Knowledge*

Next, from personal and nonpersonal communication channels, potential consumers will gather a foundation of knowledge that can be used to form beliefs about the product. For example, I believe the destination will be fun, will help reduce my stress, is convenient, and is relatively inexpensive.
  - *Marketer's Task.* Know actual and potential customers' existing beliefs about the product/brand—*what* are their beliefs. This knowledge will form the basis for understanding attitude.

- *Attitude*

As actual and potential customers begin organizing their beliefs about the product/brand, they will develop attitudes toward the product/brand. Attitudes

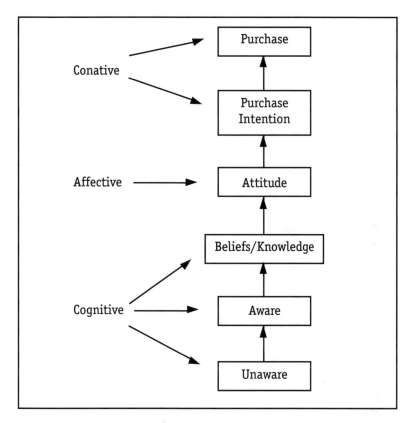

Figure 2.5: Hierarchy of effects model

Sources: Dunn, S. W., & Barban, A. M. (1978). *Advertising: Its role in modern marketing* (4th ed.). Hinsdale, Illinois: Dryden, p. 61. Lamb, C. W., Hair, J. F., Jr., & McDaniel, C. (1994). *Principles of marketing* (2nd ed.). Cincinnati: South-Western, p. 43. Sirgy, M. J. (1997). *Presentation on promotional strategies.* Blacksburg, Virginia: Virginia Tech.

that are mostly positive will lead to a global attitude of preference. A free-will purchase will not generally be made unless a consumer exhibits some level of preference for the product/brand (Sheth, Newman, & Gross, 1991). Attitudes (read, organization of beliefs) toward certain phenomena, such as one's religion, will be relatively permanent. Those surrounding phenomena with lower centrality/importance, such as restaurant selection, will be subject to change based on the consumer's changes in habit, reference groups, or promotional offers.

- *Marketer's Task.* Develop a thorough understanding of actual and potential customers' patterns of beliefs related to the product/brand. Most importantly, why do they have them and how do these beliefs influence behavior? Subsequently, marketers will use this knowledge create promotional messages that enhance or modify customers' beliefs about the product/brand. An effective and efficient means of communicating the message must then be found.

• *Purchase Intention*

Whether consumers have or have not purchased the product, they will have some degree of inclination to purchase the product in the future. Intention is based on one or more attitudes that are salient enough to motivate the consumer to consider a purchase. The measurement of purchase intention can include categories such as none, minimal, moderate, likely, or certain.

- *Marketer's Task.* Since future behavior can never be determined with 100% accuracy, intention is the next best option. Those groups with higher levels of intention will generally be the firm's target market(s).

• *Purchase*

If the consumer's attitude is reasonably positive and intention is high, then, if the consumer is sufficiently motivated, a purchase will be made.

- *Marketer's Task.* Develop a repeat customer and attempt to increase consumption or dollars spent.

MEASUREMENT OF ATTITUDE

The majority of attitude researchers feel that the attitude structure is composed of two parts, cognitive and affect (Cohen, Fishbein, & Ahtola, 1972; Fishbein, 1967; Rosenberg, 1956; Sherif et al., 1965). *Cognitive* includes beliefs about what is positive or negative about a certain phenomena, while *affect* refers to the intensity with which the cognitive belief is supported. Abelson (1964) considers the cognitive elements as the content of an individual's belief system and affect the *structure* of the belief system. Measurement of such a broad ranging and important topic must be approached with caution. Sherif et al. (1965) proposed the following "minimum" requirements:

1. Indicators of the range of positions toward the object of the attitude that is encompassed by the individual's evaluative categories (acceptable or objectionable, in some degree).

2. Indicators of the degree of the individual's personal commitment to his own stand toward the object, that is, of the degree of his ego involvement with the issue.

3. Ways and means to ensure that the individual responds in terms of his attitude toward the object rather than with what he thinks the investigator or other persons conceive as a socially desirable response. The most obvious way to avoid the latter is, of course, to use procedures that elicit attitudes without the subject's awareness. (pp. 20-21)

In order to study an individual's unbiased attitude on a topic, it is important that he or she not be informed verbally or through implicit messages (details of the topic) of the purpose of the questionnaire. Also, momentary responses to a personally administered questionnaire, as alluded to in requirement 3 above, may not reflect an individual's attitude. For example, a quick response may simply be an attempt to be viewed as a socially concerned or ethical member of society. This type of response bias, normally referred to as social desirability, is generally attributed to Edwards (1957, cited in Sherif et al., 1965).

Acceptance, Rejection, and Noncommitment

The primary components of attitude measurement are acceptance, a positive position, rejection, a negative position, and noncommitment/neutrality, neither a positive or negative position (Sherif et al., 1965). To improve the accuracy with which individuals' positions are measured, Sherif et al. offered the following assumptions and recommendations: (1) The categories in an instrument should represent those positions toward an object that are taken in social life. (The instrument should include all extreme positions in a particular domain, plus a range of positions between should be included in the survey instrument. In addition to providing a broad range of options for responses, empirical research has shown that people respond differently when presented with primarily positive alternatives than when presented with both positive and negative alternatives.) (2) The subjects should be aware that the different positions exist. (3) In test-retest situations, respondents' alternatives will be ranked in the same order. (Extreme positions may be the most consistent, while more moderate positions may be less consistent. The relative distance between positions may or may not be equal.) (4) Respondents must have the latitude to respond favorably, unfavorably, or not to respond. (Occasionally, the subject will not be able to respond to a question. Forcing a response creates unreliable data.) (5) The more extreme an individual's position (cognitive belief), the greater his degree of personal involvement (affect) and the less likely his change in attitude in an experimental situation.

Measurement Categories

Individuals, through prior experience and ego involvement, may have internalized categories/measurement scales of their own (Sherif et al., 1965). These could affect discrimination and therefore create response bias if they differ significantly from those of the survey instrument. Consequently, knowing how individuals categorize their attitudes (category labels) and the number of categories used can help researchers create questionnaires that study the individual's unbiased judgment. One means of dealing with internalized scales is to allow respondents to prioritize their responses by creating categories of their own. For example, if image were being studied, various types of image associations could

> Knowing how individuals categorize their attitudes (category labels) and the number of categories used can help researchers create questionnaires that study the individual's unbiased judgment.

be grouped together. In this instance, measurement could consist of determining differences in image between different groups.

Attitude Scale Dimensionality

The question of whether a unidimensional or multidimensional scale should be used to measure attitude is a complicated one. A unidimensional scale may be appropriate if actual research utilizing the particular unidimensional scale is reliable beyond that of chance and can be assumed to be cumulative (i.e., it represents the individual's opinion on a variety of related dimensions—an ordered pattern is well established) (Guttman, 1950, cited in Sherif et al., 1965). For example, overall attitude toward a particular restaurant could be assumed to represent attitude related to a number of dimensions, such as price, quality of food, quality of service, and so forth. This, of course, assumes that attitude toward the subordinate variables is not critical to a particular line of research. For example, a unidimensional scale measuring overall destination image may not imply endorsement of the destination's image of morality.

Most attitude scales are multidimensional and are totaled to yield a *summated score* on a particular dimension (Sherif et al., 1965). While the summated score may represent the domain of the dimension, it may not provide adequate indicators of attitude or a broad understanding of the individual's attitude regarding the dimension. For example, it may successfully rank the individual relative to others; however, it will likely neglect susceptibility to change, in which direction change is most likely, degree of commitment, tolerance of the attitude of others, and the underlying structure of the individual's attitude.

Two-Construct Attitude Models

Rosenberg's model was influenced by the work of Peak and others at the University of Michigan. In 1955, Peak (cited in Mazis, Ahtola, & Klippel, 1975) said that attitude is a means-end type structure (also referred to as an expectancy-value model). Peak proposed that the affect toward an object (means) is a function of the belief or probability that the object has positive or negative consequences (expectancy) and the strength of the affect derived from those consequences (value). Rosenberg (1956) essentially quantified Peak's proposition by showing that attitude toward an object is based on (i.e., related to) expected outcomes. His model specifically stated that an individual's attitude toward an object (A_o) is the sum of the products of the perceived instrumentality of the attitude object (I_i)—belief that the object will be instrumental in achieving or blocking value state "I" and the value importance (V_i)—the significance/utility of value state "I"—in achieving satisfaction. The sum (Σ) of "n" beliefs about "A_o" refers to the number of related beliefs/responses in the individual's salience hierarchy. That is, the inclination or motivation of an individual to act is then based on the sum of the product of each of the expectancy and value relationships. This was hypothesis one in his 1956 study and was confirmed.

$$A_o = \sum_{i=1}^{n} I_i V_i$$

Another popular attitude model (also an expectancy-value model) is that of Fishbein (1967). His model is similar to Rosenberg's in that each describes attitude as a function of beliefs/instrumentality (B_i) and the value or evaluation of an expected outcome (a_i). They differ somewhat in several respects. Fishbein's came from behavioral theory, while Rosenberg's model was derived from cognitive consistency theory. Fishbein refers to attitude toward an *act*, compared to Rosenberg's attitude toward an *object*. This difference cannot be thoroughly understood from the researchers' writings because, while Fishbein does differentiate between attitude toward an object and an act, Rosenberg makes no distinction (Mazis et al., 1975). Rosenberg's beliefs include both achieving and blocking the outcome as opposed to Fishbein's focus on achievement of salient outcome only.

$$A_{act} = \sum_{i=1}^{n} B_i a_i$$

Cohen, Fishbein, and Ahtola (1972, cited in Mazis et al., 1975) developed the adequacy-importance (A-I) model. Like Rosenberg's model, the A-I model measures attitude toward an object. However, it differs in that the A-I model measures attitude as a function of the importance (P_i) of each attribute for the subject and the evaluation of whether the object possess the desired attributes (D_i). An empirical study by Mazis et al. (1975) showed that this model was superior, a higher average r^2 than either the Rosenberg or Fishbein expectancy-value models.

$$A_o = \sum_{i=1}^{n} P_i D_i$$

Single-Construct Attitude Models

Many researchers consider attitude to be composed of a single construct: beliefs (Cronin & Taylor, 1992; Nakanishi & Bettman, 1974; Mazis et al., 1975; Rokeach, 1968; Sheth et al., 1991). In general, they propose that when prediction of behavior is the objective, single beliefs alone are adequate.

Based on a literature search, Rokeach (1968) determined that the distinction between beliefs and attitudes, while not totally without merit, may not be necessary for many research needs. His justification was that since beliefs represent a predisposition to action, they inherently contain affective components [e.g., if a person does not like spinach (a belief), this person's affect/feelings toward spinach will likely be similarly negative]. Essentially, the cognitive and affective components of the attitude model are so interrelated, it may not be necessary to distinguish between the two.

Sherif et al. (1965) take a somewhat different view, focusing more on the affective, rather than cognitive, attitude components. Their position was that the processes of cognition and affect should not be separated. Only in rare cases, such as the attempt to measure physical properties, might a decision be based exclusively on cognition. As internal standards become involved, especially in measurement of socially relevant items, affective components dominate, rendering the cognitive vs. affective argument irrelevant.

In agreement, Mazis et al. (1975) recommended that for situations where *prediction* of attitudes and behavior are desired, the adequacy measure alone is superior. However, when *understanding* of attitudes or behavior is sought, the selection of a model was more difficult and varied with the relationship between the independent variables.

Concurrently, Nakanishi and Bettman (1974) in an empirical study of expectancy-value models found that there was no significant difference between the measurement of beliefs and evaluation and the measurement of beliefs alone. In fact, their study showed that "no significant improvement in the explanatory power resulted from the inclusion of more than the most important attribute" (p. 20). While their article is one of the first to suggest a beliefs-only attitude measurement (single-scale measurement), their work has been substantiated by others such as Cronin and Taylor (1992), Mazis et al. (1975), and Sheth et al. (1991).

The adequacy-importance model (performance times weight) was tested by Cronin and Taylor (1992) in their SERVPERF article. Among the results of their empirical study was that performance measurement alone was superior to performance times weight. Cronin and Taylor studied the differences between discomfirmation and performance measures of service quality. (Discomfirmation is most associated with Oliver [Oliver & DeSarbo, 1988, cited in Oliver & Swan, 1989].)

MODELS USED IN CRONIN AND TAYLOR'S COMPARISON

Disconfirmation-Based Models
Service Quality = (Performance - Expectations)
Service Quality = Importance * (Performance - Expectations)
Performance-Based Models
Service Quality = (Performance)
Service Quality = Importance * (Performance)

$$A_o = \sum_{i=1}^{n} B_i$$

$[(A_o$ = attitude toward an object; B_i = beliefs (performance)$)]$

ENDNOTES

[1] Although conative is frequently tied to cognitive and affective perceptions, it is actually the result of the latter two constructs and therefore a separate concept.

[2] Induced image agents are also referred to a formal agents or sources of information, while organic agents are referred to as informal sources of information (Mansfeld, 1992).

[3] Heider's (1946) *balance theory* is a less sophisticated version of cognitive dissonance.

[4] Action dilemmas refer to determining a course of action—an external response.

3
Marketing Theory and Conceptualizations of the Positioning Process

SINCE POSITIONING is a component of business-level strategy, this research will begin with a review of marketing theory of the firm as proposed by Howard (1983). Even though Howard used the term *firm,* his conceptualization of marketing can apply to any marketing-oriented entity. This seminal article provides a descriptive model to help guide management in making strategy decisions. Since he states, based on empirical research, that successful firms are more likely to be customer-oriented than unsuccessful firms, marketing research establishes the basis for business-level strategy decisions. Another excellent article by Wind and Robertson (1983) is also reviewed because of its conceptual support for the positioning concept.

In addition to the apparent void in research literature on the topic of positioning (discussed in Chapter 1), there seems to be a variety of views on what constitutes the positioning process—the way positioning is planned. To help examine this situation, research was undertaken on the process of positioning. To position a product or service in the market, the firm must, as in planning of any type, have a plan or process to guide it. Therefore, included is a summary of existing positioning processes proposed by leading authors on the topic.

MARKETING THEORY AND POSITIONING— JOHN A. HOWARD

Howard (1983) proposed that since successful firms are generally customer-oriented, marketing should serve as the basis for strategy decisions. The impetus for his model of marketing theory was that since marketers are the primary resource in the firm[1] with an understanding of the customer, their input should be better utilized in setting strategy. The model is actually a superstructure composed of four elements: supply and demand, product hierarchy, competitive structure, and a customer decision model. The reason this model is interesting is that it appears to do exactly what Howard professes, guide management in making the difficult business-level strategy decisions—decisions that set the foundation for positioning.

Demand and Supply

The demand side as proposed by Howard not only specifies the customer response based on the type of product offered, but also considers how that response will vary over the product life cycle (see Figure 3.1). For example, a new product in any category (convenience, shopping, or specialty) may require a more critical review than existing offerings. The supply response shows potential questions/situations faced by various functional departments in the firm over the life cycle of the product. Because of the dynamics of competitor offerings and customer responses, there is no standardized set of strategies that can be targeted at a specific point in the product life cycle. The key point made by Howard is that it is the customer who dominates supply decisions. The research of Abernathy and Utterback (1978) on the success of product innovators was used to support Howard's contention of customer dominance of strategic decisions. While some, as Howard stresses, could say that the two sides are mutually interdependent, suppliers who best serve the customer have the best chances for survival and success.

> *This finding leads to the assumption that marketing innovation and therefore marketing's role in strategic planning is critical not only during the introduction phase of the product life cycle, but through each phase of the cycle.*

A significant point about being customer-driven is that this effort must not be viewed as being predominantly focused on the introductory segment of the product life cycle. The research of Abernathy and Utterback highlighted the fact that the sum of incremental changes to a product was generally greater than the initial R&D necessary to bring the product to market. This finding leads to the assumption that marketing innovation and therefore marketing's role in strategic planning is critical not only during the introduction phase of the product life cycle, but through each phase of the cycle.

Product Hierarchy

The product hierarchy presents a picture of a typical customer's thought process as he or she is considering a purchase (see Figure 3.2). The general purpose of the framework is to increase the opportunity for a rational purchase decision. Many concepts are incorporated in the hierarchy, such as the opportunity and/or consid-

A Customer Response	B Supplier Response

Routinized Response Behavior
1. Limited information required
2. Information content
   (a) reminder
   (b) some brand preference
3. Information form irrelevant
4. Almost no time necessary
5. Price elasticity <1; cross-elasticity high
 	
Limited Problem Solving
1. Substantial amount of information necessary
2. Information content is brand only
   (a) how brand identified
   (b) how brand performs
   (c) brand distinctiveness, information consistency, and peer consensus
3. Information form requirements loose
4. Not much time required
5. Price elasticity >1; cross-elasticity low
6. Segments develop
 	
Extensive Problem Solving
1. Great amount of information essential
2. Information content
   (a) how product is used, relation to other products
   (b) identifying and evaluative attributes
   (c) position of brand on attributes
      (1) how brand identified
      (2) how brand performs
      (3) brand distinctiveness, information consistency, and peer consensus
3. Information form: small pieces, ordered as listed, concrete, kernel sentences
4. Substantial time necessary
5. Price elasticity <1; cross-elasticity = 0
	Stable—Operations Dominated
	1. Price competition and cost reduction
	2. Cost reduction and quality improvement pressures cause process innovation
	3. Incremental process change increases quality and productivity
	4. Production capital intensive and rigid
	5. Organization control by structure, goals, and rules
	
	Transition—Product Dominated
	1. Compete on product variation, dominant design emerges
	2. Reduced customer and technical uncertainty stimulates R&D increases
	3. Major process changes required by rising volume and emerging market niches
	4. Production more rigid and changes only in major steps
	5. Organization control through liaison, project, and task groups
	
	Fluid—Market Dominated
	1. Innovation springs from customers' needs
	2. Compete on product performance
	3. Frequent major changes in product
	4. Production flexible and inefficient
	5. Organization information informal and entrepreneurial

Figure 3.1:
Demand and supply cycle

Source: Howard, J. A. (1983). Marketing theory of the firm. *Journal of Marketing, 47*(4), 90-100.

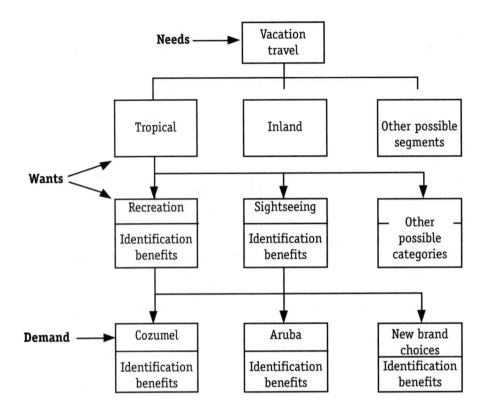

Figure 3.2:
Product hierarchy for vacation travel

Adapted from: Howard, J. A. (1983). Marketing theory of the firm. *Journal of Marketing 47*(4), p. 94.

eration set for particular needs and wants, the position of potential options, relationships among the options, and the process of selecting a preferred product.

The specific purpose is to serve as a vehicle for comparing existing options or new products to those committed to memory. The customer determines which products in the hierarchy are closest to the considered option, thereby providing information with which to form comparisons. This particular process can also provide management with information about whether a new product is in fact an innovation or simply a new brand in an existing market segment. Howard adds that market segments are created based on the relationship between the position of the customer's preferred brand to that of the typical brand as perceived by the customer.

Competitive Structure

Through the product hierarchy, management can determine who its major competitors are (Figure 3.3). This fact lends further support to the hypothesis that successful businesses are customer-driven. A problem with Howard's model of com-

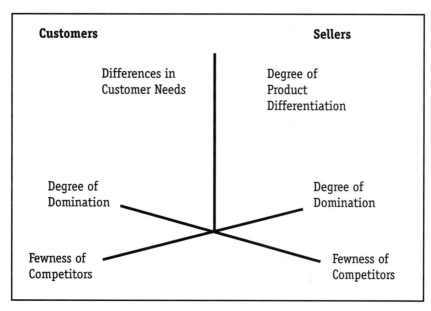

Figure 3.3:
Competitive structure

Source: Howard, J. A. (1983). Marketing theory of the firm. *Journal of Marketing 47*(4), p. 95.

petitive structure is that the model does not explain the relationships between elements and, unfortunately, only a superficial explanation is offered in the text of the article. This explanation is that the four key elements of the model are the number of competitors, size, distribution, and degree of product differentiation. He does say that his model covers much the same ground as Porter's 1980 forces of competition, so this gives the reader recourse for an explanation. From the seller's perspective, Howard says that the fewness of competitors and degree of domination are irrelevant since there are potentially millions of customers without power to influence market dynamics; however, he does not explain his reasoning. He essentially ends this discussion by saying that differences in customer needs establish market segments, that customers and suppliers determine profit margins, and that customer price elasticity influences pricing strategies.

Customer Decision Model

The customer decision model (CDM) shows how the customer thinks and processes information (Figure 3.4). Since the constructs in this model dictate a customer's purchase decision, it emphasizes the power of the customer and therefore an additional justification for being a customer-driven firm. Howard says that this particular model is "bare-bones" and can be expanded with the addition of other constructs. The CDM provides much of the information necessary for the customer portion of the supply and demand model and can be concurrently developed with the product hierarchy. It obviously also relates to the competitive struc-

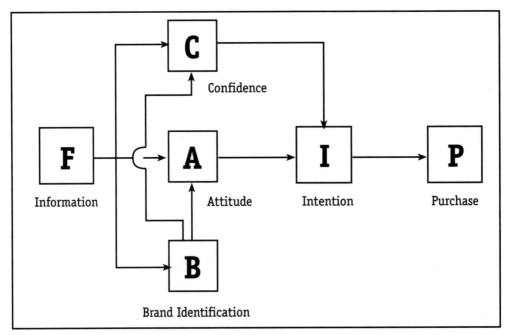

Figure 3.4:
Customer decision model

Source: Howard, J. A. (1983). Marketing theory of the firm. *Journal of Marketing* 47(4), p. 97.

ture in that information, confidence, attitude, and brand identification are highly influenced by alternative offerings.

Relationship of the Four Models

The CDM is the primary source of information for the demand side of the demand and supply cycle, the product hierarchy, and the customer side of the competitive structure. The product hierarchy supplies information for the customer side of the demand and supply cycle and competitive structure model. After the competitive structure is complete, it supplies information to the supplier side of the demand and supply cycle. Though this model is sequential in nature, in practice it is highly interactive. As changes, whether controllable or noncontrollable in nature, in any one element of a model occur, other elements of each of the models may need to be modified.

Strategic Choice

While the superstructure of the marketing theory model describes how strategy is designed, it does not prescribe how strategy should be developed (see Figure 3.5). Howard specifies that the criteria for choice is the firm's objective, generally specified as some type of maximization of the firm's resources. Since it is beyond the ability of management to compute optimal choices, maximization can only be accepted as an ideal state. Perhaps the most viable means of computing maximization is the application of the financial concept of present value. This method would require the marketer to estimate future cash flows which would serve as input for financial models that would then estimate future stock values.

Marketing theory of the firm graphically describes how strategy is set and how the different functional departments must work together to create strategy. It also shows the importance of marketing in seeking innovative strategic choices and the means for assessing their potential. Operations is seen as a rather mechanical process that can be accomplished by rational thought processes. Marketing, on the other hand, is what sets businesses apart from their cohorts.

YORAM WIND AND THOMAS S. ROBERTSON

In their 1983 article, "Market Strategy: New Directions for Theory and Research," Wind and Robertson expressed disappointment with the progress of marketing in strategy development. They felt that too much of the focus of marketing was on marketing management (decisions related to marketing mix variables). Their primary addition to marketing theory was a supplement to the traditional strategic planning process, the strategic marketing dimension (See Section II of Figure 3.6). This portion of their planning model is supported by the analyses in Figures 3.7 and 3.8. Figure 3.7 is a segment by positioning process/matrix that served as the basis for product and market selection, synergy between possible segments, functional requirements, and portfolio selection. Basically, market segments are selected and identified by their specific positioning requirements. Each of the segment/positions are then placed on a business strength/industry attractiveness-type matrix (demand in Figure 3.2). Synergy is determined through a simple matrix, by comparing the segment/positions (S#P#) to each other, and rating the degree of synergy between the various segment/positions (- = negative, + = positive).

	S1P1	S2P2	S2P3
S1P1	X	+1	+3
S2P2	-2	X	+2
S2P3	-1	-3	X

Functional requirement analysis (Figure 3.3 and Figure 3.1) includes an assessment of the ability of each functional department to meet the requirements of potential segment/positions. For example, if a certain segment/positioning is price sensitive, then purchasing, R&D, and operations management may be areas in which the business must have relative strengths. The upper-left portion of Figure 3.3 highlights overall strengths and weaknesses of the firm relative to the demands (opportunities and threats) of a specific market. The lower-left side does the same except it exposes the strength of each functional area relative to the demands of several markets. The authors do not explain the purpose of the right side of the figure. Since it is titled *Marketing Response Functions,* it could be assumed to specify which functional areas are most critical to each segment/positioning. Figure 3.9 is an overview of the authors' recommended process.

The main addition to marketing strategy of Wind and Robertson's portfolio analysis is that they take a much more sophisticated view of the decision-making

Demand and Supply Cycle

A
Customer Response

Routinized Response Behavior
1. Limited information required
2. Information content
   (a) reminder
   (b) some brand preference
3. Information form irrelevant
4. Almost no time necessary
5. Price elasticity <1; cross-elasticity high

Limited Problem Solving
1. Substantial amount of information necessary
2. Information content is brand only
   (a) how brand identified
   (b) how brand performs
   (c) brand distinctiveness, information consistency, and peer consensus
3. Information form requirements loose
4. Not much time required
5. Price elasticity >1; cross-elasticity low
6. Segments develop

Extensive Problem Solving
1. Great amount of information essential
2. Information content
   (a) how product is used, relation to other products
   (b) identifying and evaluative attributes
   (c) position of brand on attributes
      (1) how brand identified
      (2) how brand performs
      (3) brand distinctiveness, information consistency, and peer consensus
3. Information form: small pieces, ordered as listed, concrete, kernel sentences
4. Substantial time necessary
5. Price elasticity <1; cross-elasticity =0

B
Supplier Response

Stable—Operations Dominated
1. Price competition and cost reduction
2. Cost reduction and quality improvement pressures cause process innovation
3. Incremental process change increases quality and productivity
4. Production is capital intensive and rigid
5. Organization control by structure, goals, and rules

Transition—Production Dominated
1. Compete on product variation, dominant design emerges
2. Reduced customer and technical uncertainty stimulates R&D increases
3. Major process changes required by rising volume and emerging market niches
4. Production more rigid and changes only in major steps
5. Organization control through liaison, project, and task groups

Fluid—Market Demand
1. Innovation springs from customers' needs
2. Compete on product performance
3. Frequent major changes in product
4. Production flexible and inefficient
5. Organization information informal and entrepreneurial

Competitive Structure

Customers   Sellers

Difference in Customer Needs   Difference of Product Segmentation

Degree of Domination   Degree of Domination

Product Hierarchy for Restaurants

Fewness of Competitors   Fewness of Competitors

Customer Decision Model

Needs → Food

Fast-food | Casual dining | Other possible segments

Wants

Burgers Identification benefits | Chicken Identification benefits | Other possible categories

Demand → McDonald's Identification benefits | Burger King Identification benefits | Other possible categories

C
Confidence
F — A — I — P
Information   Attitude   Intention   Purchase
B
Brand Identification

Source: Wind, Y., & Robertson, T. S. (1983). Marketing strategy: New directions for theory and research. *Journal of Marketing, 47*(2), 16.

Figure 3.5:
Marketing theory of the firm

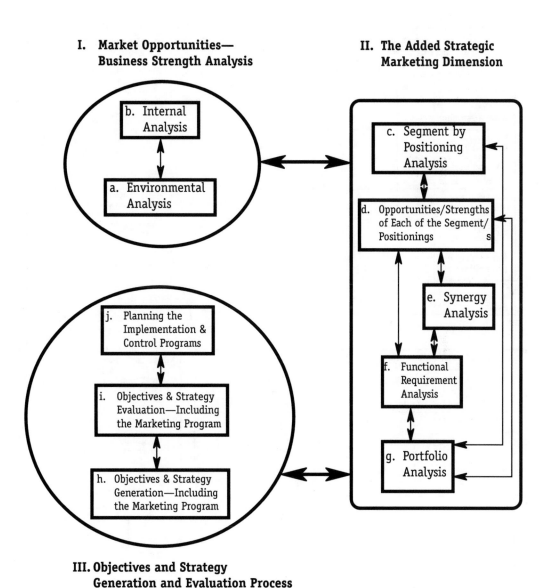

Figure 3.6:
A marketing-oriented approach to strategy formulation and evaluation

Source: Wind, Y., & Robertson, T. S. (1983). Marketing strategy: New directions for theory and research. *Journal of Marketing, 47*(2), 16.

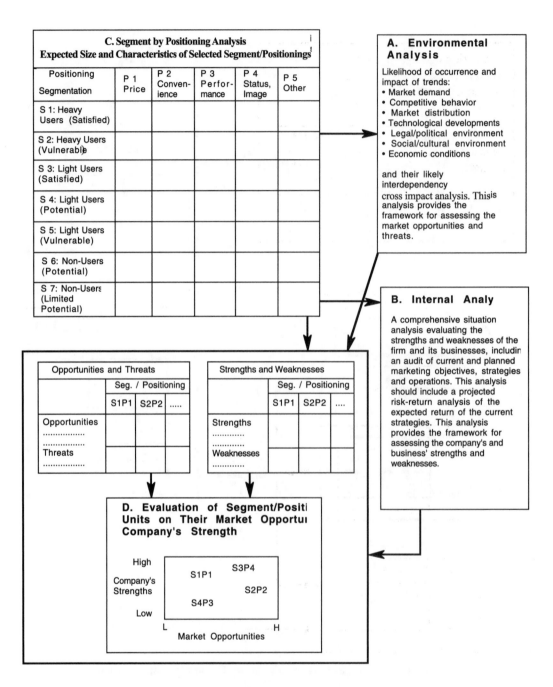

Figure 3.7:
Illustrative market opportunities and business
strength analysis by segment positioning

Source: Wind, Y., & Robertson, T. S. (1983). Marketing strategy: New directions for theory and research. *Journal of Marketing, 47*(2), 18.

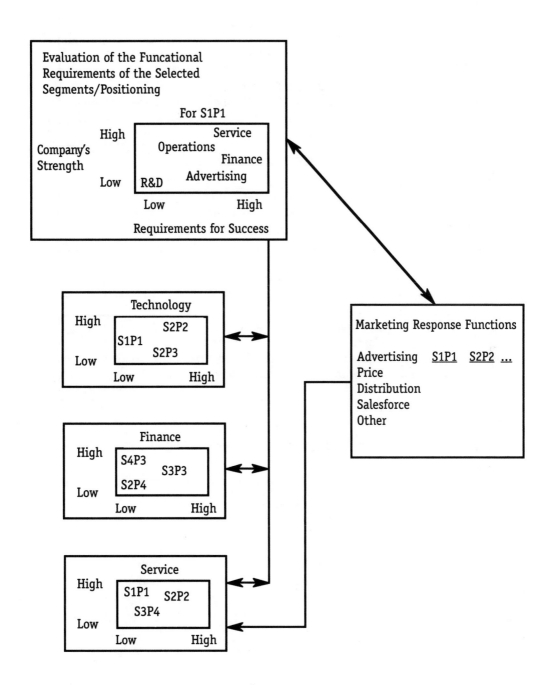

Figure 3.8:
Illustrative analysis of functional requirements

Source: Wind, Y., & Robertson, T. S. (1983). Marketing strategy: New directions for theory and research. *Journal of Marketing, 47*(2), 19.

Objectives and Strategy Generation:

Generation of:
  A. Corporate SBU and marketing objectives
  B. Strategy regarding:
      • New product and market development or acquisition
      • Selected positioning/segmentations
      • Competitive strategies
      • Marketing program (product, price, promotion, advertising, distribution, etc.)
      • Required financial, human, and material resources

Objectives and Strategy Evaluation:
  • Expected performance on key objectives
  • Impact on other functions of the firm
  • Likely market response and performance (conditional forecast given various changes in our strategy, competitive strategies, and environmental conditions)
  • Integrated evaluation (using computer planning simulation)

Planning for Implementation and Control:
  Design of adaptive experimentation program, planning continuous monitoring system, design of contingency plans, and planning of an implementation program including a time and cost CPM.

Figure 3.9:
Objective and strategy generation and evaluation

Source: Wind, Y., & Robertson, T. S. (1983). Marketing strategy: New directions for theory and research. *Journal of Marketing, 47*(2), 19.

process than do related models, such as the BCG and McKinsey/GE matrices. Essentially a separate strategic marketing plan is prepared for each actual and potential business. The "well-being" of the firm is assessed according to different scenarios: status quo—pessimistic, and optimistic; criteria—profit, risk, and maximum synergy; and strategies—product, market, and distribution. In each of these cases other criteria could be added.

Positioning Research

Marketing is said to have progressed through three evolutionary stages—*mass marketing* (one product for all customers), *product variety marketing* (products with a few different features were offered to increase the frequency of purchases of existing buyers), and *target marketing* (the identification of market segments that (a) buy a proportionately greater amount of a product at prices that produce a satisfactory profit for sellers) or (b) a business will tailor a product for, (Kotler & Armstrong, 1990). Since positioning is based on segmentation and the target-marketing process (Boyd & Walker, 1990; Lewis, Chambers, and Chacko, 1995), it is likely that the concept of positioning began some time after the more rudimentary concept of target marketing. This belief is supported by the fact that market segmentation appeared in research (Robinson, 1948) (economics research, based on the concept that some consumers have more specific demands) before market position (Alderson, 1965) and that many modern marketing writers portray positioning as a process

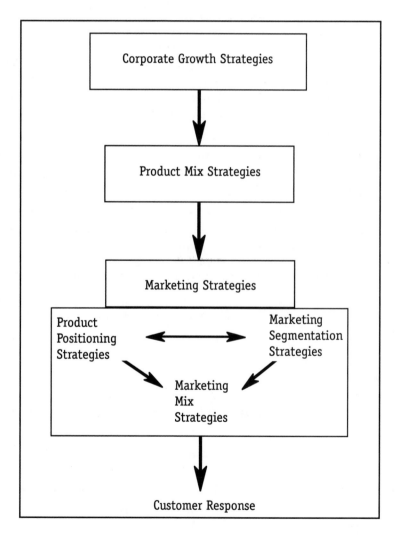

Figure 3.10:
Types of marketing strategies

Source: Assael, H. (1985). *Marketing management: Strategy and action.*
Boston: Kent, p. 113.

that follows market segmentation and market targeting (Kotler, 1991; Peter & Donnelly, 1991; Ring, Newton, Borden, & Farris, 1989; Urban & Star, 1991).

Research from the decades of the 1920s to 1970s was reviewed in an attempt to locate significant indirect references (development clues) and direct references for the topic of positioning. While the term *position* did show up in 1957 (Alderson) and *market position* in 1965 (Alderson), its action form, positioning, did not make an appearance until the 1980s. For sake of brevity, only the 1980s research will be presented.

The following sources were selected based on their strategic marketing orientation and the significance of their contribution to the topic of positioning. Because of the similarity of content, some excellent references were not included. Both generic marketing books and those focused on the hospitality industry are included.

ASSAEL

In his 1985 text, the author refers to positioning in the context of "product positioning." Product positioning is referred to in several places in his textbook, but the total allotted space is about four pages. He defines product positioning as "the set of product benefits that management wants to convey to a defined target segment to meet its needs" (Assael, 1985, p. 43). He views marketing strategies as consisting of product-positioning strategies, marketing segmentation strategies, and marketing-mix strategies. A product can be positioned according to various benefits, such as attributes and features, problem solutions, emotional attachment, occasions for use, price and value, and by comparing it to a competing product offering (essentially, needs and competition or uniqueness). Before marketing-mix strategies can be selected, the product positioning and market segmentation decisions must be made (see Figure 3.10). Without these decisions, marketing strategies will be "ill defined and the brand is likely to fail" (Assael, 1985, p. 103). In a few brief paragraphs on service positioning, he says that this task is more difficult than product positioning because of "the need to communicate vague and intangible benefits" (Assael, 1985, p. 716).

BOYD AND WALKER

In *Marketing Management: A Strategic Approach* (1990), Boyd and Walker present the most thorough coverage of positioning of any of the authors researched. Positioning is included in Chapter 10, "Market Targeting and Positioning Decisions." It is in Section II of the book, *Market Opportunity Analysis,* which covers marketing research and topics related to the environment. The subsequent Section III, entitled "Developing Strategic Marketing Programs," is concerned with business-level generic strategies and the 4Ps of marketing.

In their "Market Targeting and Positioning Decisions" chapter, the authors begin by offering definitions of the two terms: "market targeting—determining which segment or segments within a market the firm will direct its marketing efforts toward" and "market positioning—designing a marketing program and product that a segment's customers will perceive as desirable, and that will give the firm a differential advantage over current and potential competitors" (Boyd & Walker, 1990, p. 315). They then commingle the terms in describing the processes of market targeting and positioning.

Evaluating Target Markets

Few firms utilize mass markets; most will divide the market up into segments with homogeneous requirements. Since each segment will vary in its potential for sales, profit, stability, growth, and longevity, each must be prioritized in some manner. Managers will then create marketing programs (products, prices, place, and promotion) designed to attract chosen segments.

To assure a commonality of understanding between various business-level managers within a corporation, the authors recommend the use of a market attractiveness/business position matrix (commonly referred to as a business strength/industry attractiveness matrix). While this matrix is normally used in corporate portfolio analysis for resource allocation of businesses within a parent firm, it can be adapted for a single firm (it can be likewise used to analyze competitors). The five steps for creating the matrix are described below (see Figure 3.11).

1. *Measurement criteria.* The criteria or factors for assessing market attractiveness and competitive position are derived from the internal and environmental analyses. Their selection for any specific firm is based on their ability to affect the firm's success. Boyd and Walker (1990) include the following factors for measuring market attractiveness and competitive position:

MARKET ATTRACTIVENESS FACTORS
Market/customer factors
>Size (dollars, units)
>Market potential
>Market growth rate
>Stage in life cycle
>Diversity of competitive offerings
>>(potential for differentiation)
>Customer loyalty/satisfaction
>>with current offerings
>Price elasticity
>Bargaining power of customers
>Cyclicality/seasonality of demand

1. Choose criteria to measure attractiveness and competitive position.

2. Weight attractiveness and competitive position factors to reflect their relative importance.

3. Assess the current position of each potential target market on each factor.

4. Project the future position of each market based on expected environmental, customer, and competitive needs.

5. Evaluate implications of possible future changes for business strategies and resource requirements.

Figure 3.11:
Steps in construction of a market attractiveness/business position matrix for evaluating potential target markets

Source: Boyd, H. W., Jr., & Walker, O. C., Jr. (1990). *Marketing management: A strategic approach.* Homewood, Illinois: Irwin, p. 317.

Economic and technological factors
    Investment intensity
    Industry capacity
    Level and maturity of technology utilization
    Ability to pass through effects of inflation
    Barriers to entry/exit
    Access to raw materials
Competitive factors
    Industry structure
    Competitive groupings
    Substitution threats
    Perceived differentiation among competitors
    Individual competitors' strengths

Environmental factors
>Regulatory climate
>Degree of social acceptance

COMPETITIVE POSITION FACTORS
Market position factors
>Relative market share
>Rate of change in share
>Perceived actual or potential differentiation
>>(quality/service/price)
>Breadth of current or planned product line
>Company image

Economic and technological factors
>Relative cost position
>Capacity utilization
>Technological position
>Patented technology (product or manufacturing)

Capabilities
>Management strength and depth
>Financial
>R&D/product development
>Manufacturing
>Marketing
>Salesforce
>Distribution system
>Labor relations
>Relations with regulators

Interactions with other segments
>Market synergies
>Operating synergies (p. 318)

2. *Weighting of the criteria.* Since factors are rarely of equal importance, a weighted measurement scale is used to place a heavier emphasis on more critical factors. The authors present a scale based on a random total number of points, 450 (i.e., 9 factors with a rating scale of 1—very unattractive to 5—very attractive, and a weighting scale of 1—unimportant to 10—very important, 9 x 5 x 10 = 450). A rating is derived for market attractiveness and competitive position.[2]

3. *Assessing the business's position in the matrix.* This step is simply to locate the coordinates on the matrix (see Figure 3.12). The size of the circle represents the actual or potential sales for the market segment. The arrow is discussed below.

4. *Projection of future growth.* Forecasting future market attractiveness and competitive position is considerably more speculative than assessing current performance. To allow for the uncertainty of forecasting, several scores for each construct (market and position) could be developed using scenario analysis. A vector (arrow) can be

Competitive position

	Strong	Medium	Weak

Figure 3.12:
Location in the market attractiveness/business position matrix

Source: Boyd, H. W., Jr., & Walker, O. C., Jr. (1990). *Marketing management: A strategic approach.* Homewood, Illinois: Irwin, p. 32.

used to plot the forecasted movement for the analysis. In the example in Figure 3.12, the market is expected to become more attractive and the firm's competitive position is expected to weaken slightly as more firms enter the market.

5. *Evaluation of implications of changing corporate strategies to pursue a chosen market.* The authors recommend choosing a segment with a combination of at least one highly positive coordinate and one medium coordinate. The selection of a market with a lesser score should be considered only if the market's attractiveness or firm's competitive position are expected to improve in the future, the market is viewed as a stepping stone to a more attractive market, or where synergies exist. Resources should be concentrated in attractive markets where the firm is well positioned, used to improve the firm's weak position in attractive markets, and generally not allocated to remaining locations in the matrix.

Steps in the Positioning Process

The authors offer the following steps for determining existing perceptions and the positioning decision for a new product or the repositioning of a current product (see Figure 3.13).

1. *Competitive products.* The positioning analysis should include both product-category and brand-level analyses (see Figure 3.14). The product-category level includes various products viewed as substitutes for the product a business's management is attempting to position (Figure 3.14A). For example, an all-suites hotel

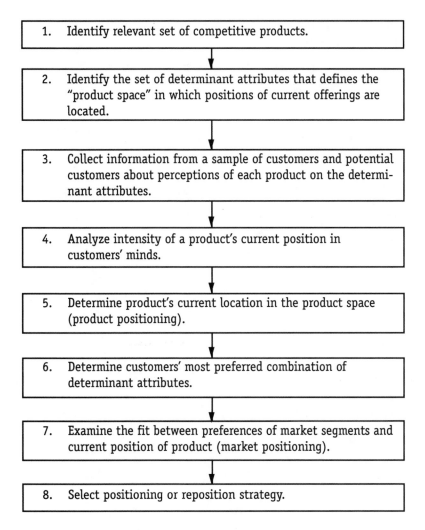

Figure 3.13:
Steps in the positioning process

ource: Boyd, H. W., Jr., & Walker, O. C., Jr. (1990). *Marketing management: A strategic approach.* Homewood, Illinois: Irwin, p. 329.

could be considered as a substitute by some market segments for upper/midscale properties. The brand-level analysis is concerned with how the business's brand is viewed on various important attributes compared to competing brands (Figure 3.14B). This analysis helps locate strengths and weaknesses relative to the competition and potentially viable or more suitable positions based on the business's abilities.

2. *Identify determinant attributes.* To create the positioning maps in step #1, determinant attributes must be identified. This can be accomplished by the use of various types of statistical techniques. While some attributes, such as soap in an upper-midscale hotel property may be important, they are generally not critical in the decision of where to stay. Determinant attributes, therefore, are those that have the greatest influence on choice.

**A. Product category positions
(Breakfast foods market)**

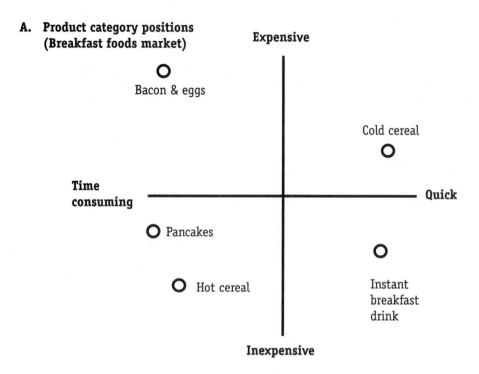

**B. Brand positions
(Instant breakfast market)**

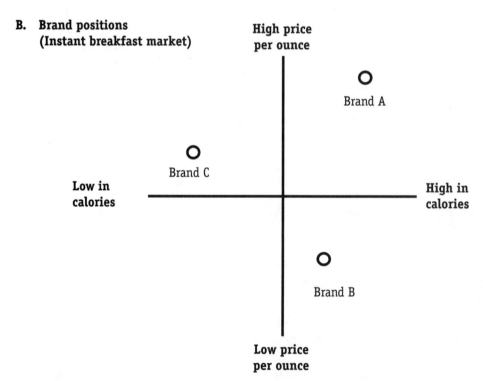

Figure 3.14:
Product category and brand positioning

ource: Boyd, H. W., Jr., & Walker, O. C., Jr. (1990). *Marketing management: A strategic approach.* Homewood, Illinois: Irwin, p. 331.

3. *Determine customers' perceptions.* Techniques such as factor analysis, discriminant analysis, multiattribute compositional models, and multidimensional scaling are common techniques used to identify perceptions. The authors recommend multidimensional scaling (perceptual maps) because of its ability to identify underlying attributes without a priori assumptions.

4. *Intensity of current position.* Ries and Trout are referenced as saying that the marketer's objective is to achieve "an intense, distinctive position for a brand so that it is thought of first and evaluated as the best brand on at least one determinant attribute by customers preparing to make a purchase" (Boyd & Walker, 1990, p. 333). The first step in assessing intensity is to find out which brand is thought of first for a specific product category (e.g., fast-food restaurants). This is generally referred to as top-of-mind awareness and is by measuring the average ranking of competing brands through unaided recall. The brand should also rank high on the various determinant attributes assessed by target market before making a purchase.

Normally, management should not focus on more than one, or perhaps up to three, attributes, especially for low-involvement products that customers spend little time thinking about (e.g., fast-food or convenience products). Additionally, if a competitor is already strongly positioning in an important attribute, management will likely need to select another attribute to focus on.

A constraint or problem with establishing a strong position is that the markets' preferences may change, making it difficult for the business to change its position. For example, a business is strongly positioned on value, a determinant attribute. A change in the market occurs and quality becomes the dominant attribute. A considerable advertising budget may be necessary to convince customers that the business can produce a quality product when the focus had been on value.

5. *The product's current relative position.* It is recommended to measure the current position through the use of positioning maps with determinant attributes as the axes. For example, in Figure 3.14B above, Brands A, B, and C occupy different positions along the determinant attributes of calories and price. Brands that are close to one another are assumed to be viewed similarly by the target market.

This analysis also provides marketers with information about gaps in the market that are not currently being filled. This gap may represent an opportunity, if there is adequate demand.

6. *Market positioning.* Through discriminant or factor analysis and multidimensional scaling, customers are surveyed to ascertain their ideal product for any specific category. The business's product is then compared with the attributes of this ideal product.

7. *Define market positioning and market segmentation.* The market positioning map can also be used to identify market segments. In addition to the location of various brands or products on the axes, segments of customers with similar needs and wants can be identified. If most customers cluster around one point on the positioning map, there is probably one segment for the applicable variables. Two or more clusters denote distinct segments with different requirements. The size of the segments can be represented on the map by varying the size of a circle used for the

segment. This step helps tell marketers about how well its business and competitors are positioned to meet each segment's needs and wants, the intensity of rivalries between competitors, and the opportunity for finding a unique position in the market.

8. *Select positioning strategies.* The selection of a position should consider the preferences of market segments and the positions of competing firms. The basic choices include:

- **Monosegment Positioning:** Targeting one's marketing program to a single market segment.
- **Multisegment Positioning**: Finding a location between two segments whose needs and wants the business can satisfy.
- **Imitative Positioning:** The business can select the same position as an existing successful brand, hoping that it can attract some of its customers. Since this strategy will often bring a response from the similar competitor, businesses attempting it should have some type of competitive advantage, such as a newer concept, larger advertising budget, or a better-quality product.
- **Defensive Positioning**: If a business determines that it is vulnerable to imitation positioning, it could defend itself by introducing similar products for its current market. The purpose of this strategy would be to lower the attractiveness of its market segment.

Figure 3.15:
Functional planning serves as a basis for the strategic plan; the strategic plan sets the context for finalizing functional plans

Source: Powers, T. (1990). *Marketing hospitality.* New York: John Wiley & Sons, p. 331.

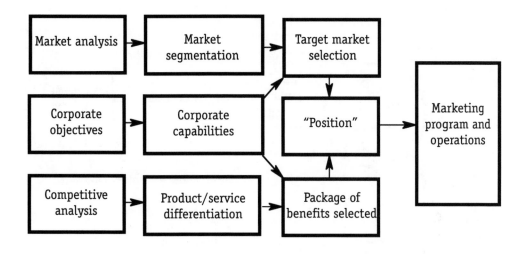

Figure 3.16: Forces at work in defining market position

Source: Powers, T. (1990). *Marketing hospitality*. New York: John Wiley & Sons, p. 331. (Developed from a concept of Michael Pearce of the University of Western Ontario.)

- **Anticipatory Positioning**: If there is currently little demand for a certain location on the positioning map, but marketers feel that demand will increase, then this position might be pursued.

POWERS

Powers (1990) gives four pages to positioning in a chapter entitled, "Marketing Planning." He refers to positioning as the "link between marketing strategy and marketing planning" (Powers, 1990, p. 325) (see Figure 3.15). Powers uses the term *market planning* as the process of setting tactics. He goes on to say that marketing planning provides input for the strategic plan (this statement is counter to his previous remarks about marketing strategies and marketing planning) and that the "company's position is the link between the long-range strategic plan and the more specific and tactical marketing plan" (Powers, 1990, p. 330).

Positioning is defined as the "process of establishing and maintaining a distinctive place in the market for an organization and/or its individual product offerings" (Powers, 1990, p. 327). This is a quote from Lovelock (1991, p. 134). Powers explains it as an attempt to match management's desire of how the business will be viewed with the resulting view of customers (see Figure 3.16).

The three key factors in the positioning decision are consumer needs, competitive offerings, and the business's resources or capabilities (see Figure 3.17). Consumer needs are identified through market segmentation. Competitive offerings are identified through an analysis of competitors' products and services, and their

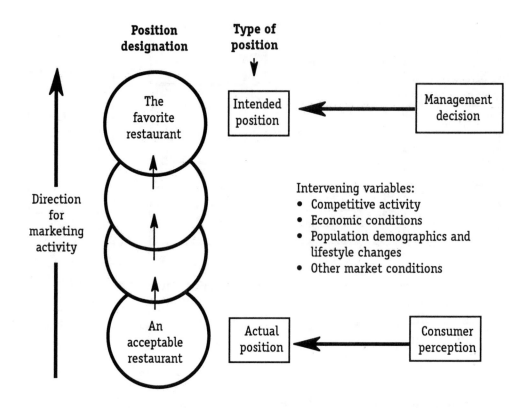

Figure 3.17:
The task of marketing: Bring an actual and intended position center

Source: Powers, T. (1990). *Marketing hospitality.* New York: John Wiley & Sons, p. 329.

strengths and weaknesses. The business's resources and objectives determine what it can attempt in the market.

The Positioning Statement

Powers does not discuss how to prepare a positioning statement, but says that it should be "an upbeat, positive statement of the company's intended position" (Powers, 1990, p. 330). Several examples are provided, one of which follows:

"Swiss Chalet is a Family Style restaurant chain that consistently offers excellent value, the best tasting chicken, and is nutrition conscious" (Powers, 1990, p. 330).

Repositioning

As customer ages and tastes change, the business must consider repositioning itself. Repositioning is defined as "a deliberate attempt to change a company's image in consumers' minds relative to its competitors; that is, to change the company's perceived position" (Powers, 1990, p. 332). He adds that repositioning may include changes in market segments, benefits offered, prices, location, and promotional strategies.

KOTLER

Kotler (1991) allots seven pages to positioning in a chapter entitled "Marketing Strategies for Differentiating and Positioning the Marketing Offer." The chapter is included in Part IV of the book *Designing Marketing Strategies.* The preceding chapter in the book, "Identifying Market Segments and Selecting Target Markets," focuses on identifying unique attributes of the target market. In a later chapter, he says that "In general, firms will occupy different competitive positions[3] in the target market" (Kotler, 1991, p. 374).

He defines differentiation and positioning as follows: "Differentiation is the act of designing a set of meaningful differences to distinguish the company's offer from competitors' offers" and "Positioning is the act of designing the company's offer so that it occupies a distinct and valued place in the target customers' minds" (Kotler, 1991, p. 302). Kotler looks upon differentiation and positioning as a linked pair of planning activities. (The definitions are virtually identical.) The first focuses on what to differentiate, the latter considers how to be promote the differences so they will be valued by target customers.

After ending the first part of the chapter's discussion on differentiation, Kotler begins the positioning section by specifying that differentiation is worth establishing as long as it satisfies the following criteria:

- **Important:** The difference delivers a highly valued benefit to a sufficient number of buyers.
- **Distinctive:** The difference either isn't offered by other or is offered in a more distinctive way by the company.
- **Superior**: The difference is superior to other ways to obtain the same benefit.
- **Communicable:** The difference is communicable and visible to buyers.
- **Preemptive:** The difference cannot be easily copied by competitors.
- **Affordable**: The buyer can afford to pay for the difference.
- **Profitable**: The company will find it profitable to introduce the difference (p. 301).

Authors Ries and Trout and Rosser Reeves are referenced as saying that a firm should select "one consistent positioning message" (Kotler, 1991) and then stick to it and heavily emphasize it. The message should be one of the firm's strengths that is highly valued by the target market. Examples of positioning messages include low price, great value, advanced technology, highest quality, and excellent service. He says that in some cases a firm may need to use double benefit positioning or triple benefit positioning. For example, if competing firms are promoting similar benefits, then an additional benefit or two could be added to the strategy. He says that firms should avoid the four major positioning errors:

- **Underpositioning**: Some companies discover that buyers have only a vague idea of the brand. Buyers don't really know anything special about it.
- **Overpositioning**: Buyers may have too narrow a picture of the brand. Thus a consumer might think that the Steuben company makes only fine glass in the range of $1,000 and up when in fact it makes affordable fine glass starting at around $50.
- **Confused Positioning:** Buyers could have a confused image of the brand. This confusion might result from making too many claims or changing the brand's positioning too frequently.
- **Doubtful Positioning:** Buyers may find it hard to believe the brand claims in view of the product's features, price, or manufacturer (p. 303).

A decision heuristic is offered, consisting of determining the firm's position on various attributes as compared to each major competitor, the importance of improving on that position, the affordability and speed with which the position can be changed, the competitors' ability to improve their position, and the recommendation of what to do for each positioning attribute (hold, improve, monitor, etc.). For example, if a firm found that it and a competitor are equally well thought of in terms of value, an important attribute for their target market, the firm has essentially two options. It can either select another attribute to promote, or the firm can promote value and one or more additional attributes. Once the positioning decision is made, then management can go on to select its marketing mix variables.

In addition to offering the above recommendations for positioning and a quasi-process (heuristic), Kotler views the marketing management process as including analyzing marketing opportunities; researching and selecting target markets; designing marketing strategies (differentiating and *positioning*, new product development, product life cycle, and *competitive positions*); planning marketing programs; and organizing, implementing, and controlling marketing effort.

Competitive positions concern a firm's place in the position relative to competing firms in its industry. Two classification schemes are provided (neither is referred to as a typology or taxonomy). One from Arthur D. Little management consulting consists of

- **Dominant:** This firm controls the behavior of other competitors and has a wide choice of strategic options.
- **Strong:** This firm can take independent action without endangering its long-term position and can maintain its long-term position regardless of competitors' actions.
- **Favorable:** This firm has a strength that is exploitable in particular strategies and has more than average opportunity to improve its position.
- **Tenable:** This firm is performing at a sufficiently satisfactory level to warrant continuing in business, but it exists at the sufferance of the dominant company and has a less-than-average opportunity to improve its position.

- **Nonviable:** This firm has unsatisfactory performance and no opportunity for improvement (p. 374).

LOVELOCK

Lovelock (1991) covers positioning in eight pages in a chapter entitled "Positioning a Service in the Marketplace." The chapter begins with a brief discourse on the differences between goods and services. He says that the tangibility of a good makes it easy for the customer to analyze it prior to use as opposed to a service that must be analyzed during its use. Positioning is defined as "the process of establishing and maintaining a distinctive place in the market for an organization and/or its individual product offerings" (Lovelock, 1991, p. 110). He notes Heskett's (1984) view that the business must separate itself from competitors by differentiating or altering common characteristics of their industry. Repositioning is defined simply as "changing the existing position" (Lovelock, 1991, p. 110).

Uses of Positioning in Marketing Management
Lovelock says that many marketers associate positioning with promotional elements of the marketing mix (which he terms "copy positioning"), thereby ignoring the overall aspects of the term (termed "product positioning"). The list below highlights the uses of positioning for "product development, service delivery, pricing, and communications strategy" (Lovelock, 1991, p. 111).

Principal Uses of Positioning in Marketing Management
I. Provide a useful diagnostic tool for defining and understanding the relationships between products and markets:
   A. How does the product compare with competitive offerings on specific attributes?
   B. How well does product performance meet consumer needs and expectations on specific performance criteria?
   C. What is the predicted consumption level for a product with a given set of performance characteristics offered at a given price?
II. Identify market opportunities for
   A. Introducing new products
      1. What segment to target?
      2. What attributes to offer relative to the competition?
   B. Redesigning (repositioning) existing products
      1. Appeal to the same segments or to new ones?
      2. What attributes to add, drop, or change?
      3. What attributes to emphasize in advertising?
   C. Eliminate products that
      1. Do not satisfy consumer needs
      2. Face excessive competition

III. Making other market mix decisions to preempt, or in response to, competitive moves:
  A. Distribution strategies
    1. Where to offer the product (locations, types of outlet)?
    2. When to make the product available?
  B. Pricing strategies
    1. How much to charge?
    2. What billing and payment procedures to employ?
  C. Communication strategies
    1. What target audience(s) are most easily convinced that the product offers a competitive advantage on attributes that are important to them?
    2. What message(s)? (Which attributes should be emphasized and which competitors—if any—should be mentioned as the basis for comparison on those attributes?)

> *As a position is selected, management must prepare for the possibility that a competitor will select the same or a similar position, and the potential reactions of that firm.*

    3. Which communication channels—person selling versus different advertising media? (Selected not only for their ability to convey the chosen message(s) to the target audience(s), but also for their ability to reinforce the desired image of the product.)

He views positioning as the link between market analysis, competitive analysis, and internal analysis (see Figure 3.18), the results of which, a positioning statement, answer the questions of "What is our product (or service concept), what do we want it to become, and what actions must we take to get there?" (Lovelock, 1991, p. 111). Positioning strategy may have to be developed for the organization, for a given outlet, or for a specific service. Failure to select a position can result in facing competition from strong competitors; being in a position with little demand; customers who do not know how the firm is positioned (why they should select it over other options); and having no position, because no one is aware of it. As a position is selected, management must prepare for the possibility that a competitor will select the same or a similar position, and the potential reactions of that firm. One way to avoid this occurrence is to perform a detailed competitor analysis, including developing or determining the likely position that may be selected by primary competitors.

Understanding Consumer Choice Behavior

Lovelock recommends the use of positioning maps to identify perceived differences in how customers view a firm or its offering. Of critical significance is the

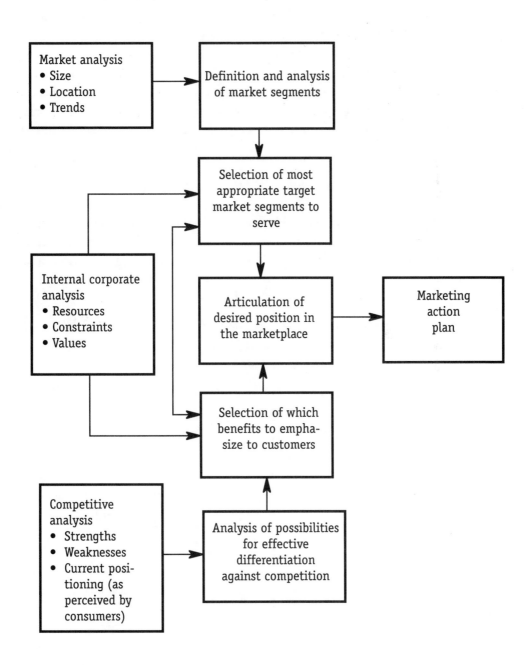

Figure 3.18:
Developing a market positioning strategy

Source: Lovelock, C. H. (1991). *Services marketing.* New York: Prentice Hall, p. 112.
(Developed by Lovelock from a work of Michael R. Pearce.)

differentiation between determinant attributes (key to determining choice) and important attributes (those that are expected and offered by most competitors). He cautions against generalizing about a particular market segment's priorities, because needs may vary for the same person based on the purpose for the purchase, who makes the decision, timing (evening, day, week, season, and so forth), whether alone or in a group, and the composition of the group. Also, some attributes are relatively easy to quantify, such as price or speed of service, but qualitative attributes, such as atmosphere, may present more of a problem.[4]

Lovelock ends with the recommendation that, because of the dynamics of the marketplace, managers need to reassess their positions.

RING, NEWTON, BORDEN, AND FARRIS

The authors' book, *Decisions in Marketing: Cases and Text* (1989), allots eight pages to positioning in a chapter entitled "Product Policy." The authors do not define positioning, but state that it is a "counterpart of market segmentation" and

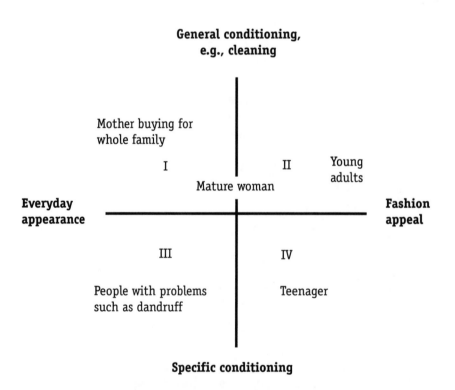

Figure 3.19: Customer types positioned in perceptual space (for shampoo)

Source: Ring, L. J., Newton, D. A., Borden, N. H. Jr., & Farris, P. W. (1989). *Decisions in marketing: Cases and text.* Homewood, Illinois: BPI Irwin, p. 304.

that "after choosing the segment to be served, a product or service desired for that segment is positioned against a segment" (Ring et al., 1989, p. 300). The majority of their focus is on creating and interpreting perceptual maps. One difference between these textbook authors and others is that in addition to recognizing plot points on the matrix, they also recommend the analysis of the quadrant (see Figure 3.20). In addition to stressing that competitors and product gaps should be located on the perceptual maps, the authors discuss the problems encountered when attempting to position one brand for several segments. While the product may be equal to or superior to competing brands, it may be difficult to get one target group, young adults, for instance, to purchase the same product that is promoted to senior citizens.

Repositioning

Repositioning is "a decision to change the segment served by a brand or to broaden the segments served or to narrow the segment served" (Ring et al., 1989, p. 305). This statement is reinforced by saying that marketers will simply attempt to move the product to a different place on the perceptual map. Repositioning is difficult because the product already has a reputation with existing customers. Therefore, attempts to convince them that the product is different than what has been promoted and experienced may not be accepted. Also, the business's skills and fi-

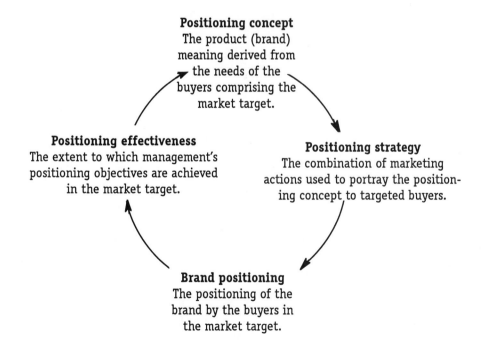

Figure 3.20:
Cravens positioning process

Source: Cravens, D. W. (1994). *Strategic marketing* (4th ed.). Burr Ridge, Illinois: Irwin, p. 305.

nancial resources should be considered for repositioning or new product introductions. Their discussion on repositioning is followed by a section entitled "Trading Down and Trading Up." Here, they say that a product can be promoted to a different segment, below or above that of the present targeted segment.

CRAVENS

In his textbook, *Strategic Marketing* (1994, 4th edition, originally published in 1982), Cravens offers a concise but reasonably detailed process. It includes (1) positioning concept, (2) positioning strategy, (3) brand positioning (explained as *determining position*), and (4) positioning effectiveness (see Figure 3.20). (Sixteen pages of text are allotted for positioning information.)

Positioning Concept

The positioning concept is how marketing managers want target customers to view their firm or any of its specific products, relative to competing firms and products. From the customers' perspective, this concerns how the firm's products meet their needs and satisfy their wants. The positioning concept is linked to customers' needs and wants by the functional, symbolic, and experiential concepts. The functional concept includes products that solve consumption-related problems. Food and a hotel room solve basic problems. The symbolic concept applies to the customer's need for ego gratification. A night at the Ritz-Carlton or dinner at the Windows on the World certainly elevate a hotel stay and meal to a level above the average individual's basic needs. Experiential concepts provide sensory or cognitive pleasure and variety. A visit to Disney World, Sea World, or Six Flags is generally viewed as quite stimulating by their patrons.

Positioning Strategy

This step coordinates the selection of marketing mix variables (product, price, place, and promotion) with the objective of achieving the positioning concept.[5] Resources must be allocated between the various strategy choices. The factors that affect the positioning strategy include the target market's specific requirements; stage in the product life cycle; management's priorities, such as grow, hold, milk, or divest; resources available to implement positioning concept; and competitors' existing and potential strategic choices. Changes in the positioning strategy are not made frequently. Generally they are considered at different stages of the product life cycle and in response to changes in the environment. A rational relationship must exist between the resources expended and the response garnered from the target market.

Determining Position

This entails locating the firm's or brand's actual position in the selected market. The purpose is to help determine future changes in the positioning strategy. The three methods provided for determining the position are customer and competitor research, with experiments being the only example; test marketing to determine commercial feasibility (cost of testing, risk associated with the venture, and likelihood of competitor reaction are also considered); and positioning models, computerized programs for decision analysis.

Positioning Effectiveness

Determining the position's effectiveness includes measurements such as market share, profit, growth rates, customer satisfaction, and other unspecified measures of competitive advantage. Quantitative measures are viewed as more objective; however, having a competitive advantage, such as a unique product, is important to consider.

LEWIS, CHAMBERS, AND CHACKO

Lewis, Chambers, and Chacko (1995) allot 35 pages to positioning in a chapter entitled "Market Positioning." According to the authors, market positioning is defined as "creating an image in the consumer's mind" (Lewis et al., 1995, p. 343). It is the next step in marketing planning after segmentation and target marketing, and sets the stage for all that occurs in the business. The objective of market positioning is create a distinctive image for the business in the minds of potential customers, one that considers the needs and wants of customers relative to competitors' offerings. Lovelock's (1991) pitfalls for businesses that do not effectively position themselves are listed. (While there is valuable information in this chapter, parts of it are questionable.)

Objective and Subjective Positioning

There are two types of positioning that are selected based on the customer and competitive situation. Objective positioning "is concerned almost entirely with the objective attributes of the physical product" (Lewis et al., 1995, p. 343), focusing on the physical product and its features—that which exists. Examples provided include the Econolodge as an inexpensive motel, the Ponderosa as selling steaks, and the Chicago Hilton as a large hotel. Image "derives from an objective, concrete, specific attribute" (Lewis et al., 1995, p. 344). In the next paragraph the authors say that objective positioning will not always be concrete. It can be abstract, such as the cleanliness of McDonald's, the Ritz-Carlton as a luxury hotel, and Lutece as serving gourmet meals and fine wines.

The idea is to select a unique characteristic or feature that can be used to objectively position the product and differentiate it from competitors. Examples provided are hotel atriums, the richness of Haagen Dazs ice cream, Red Lobster positions on seafood, and The Plaza Hotel positions on the important people that stay there.

Subjective positioning includes the non-physical attributes "as perceived by the customer—they belong not necessarily to the product but to the customer's mental perception"[6] (Lewis et al., 1995, p. 346). Since these attributes are based on individual perceptions, they may be different for each person or target group. The test of a business's subjective positioning is that customers have a positive image of the business, "whether or not the image is true"[7] (Lewis et al., 1995, p. 347). The Hilton's "America's Business Address" campaign was noted as an example of an unsuccessful attempt at subjective positioning: unsuccessful, because it was not able to differentiate Hilton from the competition.[8]

Under the heading of subjective positioning, the authors include tangible positioning and intangible position. For tangible positioning, since the hospitality industry is reaching a point of saturation and the product is rather generic, marketers must develop "intangible mental perceptions that may or may not actually belong to the product" (Lewis et al., 1995, p. 347). Optional strategies for positioning the tangible and undifferentiated hospitality product included focusing on fun, people, and convenience.

Intangible positioning is the concept that the industry is marketing the intangible, even though it does sell a tangible product—rooms and food. What has to be done is to tangibilize intangible aspects of the business. For example, the Hyatt's atriums represent excitement; Merrill Lynch's bull tangibilizes the intangible benefits of investing through their firm.

> *Repositioning is attempting to create a new position for the business and is essentially the same as positioning with the exception of having to deal with the business's existing position.*

Effective Positioning

Effective positioning "must promise the benefit the customer will receive, it must create the expectation, and it must offer a solution to the customer's problem" (Lewis et al., 1995, p. 351). The solution should be unique in some way and better than the competition. The authors then go on to say, "Here are some better-known positioning statements," without a discussion of what positioning statements are. Some examples include Toyota's "I love what you do for me," Hyatt's "Feel the Hyatt touch," Burger King's "Have it your way," and others.[9]

Repositioning

Repositioning is attempting to create a new position for the business and is essentially the same as positioning with the exception of having to deal with the business's existing position. Repositioning may be necessary for a variety of reasons, such as having selected a less than viable position, not having attained the selected position, competitors having made the position less attractive, or the desire to add new target markets. The procedure for repositioning includes:
- Determine the present position.
- Determine what position you wish to occupy.

- Make sure the product is truly different for the repositioning.
- Initiate the repositioning campaign based on the three criteria of effective positioning formulated from the research of the target market: image, differentiation, and promised benefits.
- Remeasure to see if the position has significantly changed in the desired direction.

Developing Positioning Strategies

For developing positioning strategies, Lewis et al. recommend the use of the Michael Pearce model as printed in Lovelock's (1991) marketing textbook and Aaker & Shansby's (1982) approaches for selecting positioning strategies.

Salience, Determinance, and Importance

Lewis et al. noted that consideration of attributes or benefits should be based on whether they are salient, determinant, or important. Salient attributes are those that are on the top of the mind, the characteristics that are first thought of when someone considers a purchase. However, these are not necessarily what customers will base their decisions on. Determinant attributes are those attributes used to signal choice. For example, a hotel's location may be salient, but its service may be the determinant attribute. Important attributes are those that are generally expected and offered by most competitors. Amenities are important, but since most hospitality firms in any one market segment have those that are considered important, they do not determine choice.

The authors go on to discuss competitive positioning by using perceptual maps and internal positioning. They recommend that, in addition to analyzing competitors that are closely associated with one's business, other similar competitors be examined for possible opportunities. Also, an ideal place on the map is located to help locate "gaps or niches or, conversely, the crowded areas" (Lewis, et al., 1995, p. 364). Finally, they say that internal positioning is important and deals with internal aspects of the business such as the decor, occasions for purchase, and value.

KOTLER, BOWEN, AND MAKENS

Kotler, Bowen, and Makens (1996) allot six pages for positioning. They view positioning as following segmentation and target marketing and define it as "the way the product is defined by consumers on important attributes—the place the product occupies in consumers' minds relative to competing products" (Kotler et al., 1996, p. 259). Since customers do not have the time to evaluate products each time a purchase is made, they perceptually position products based on how well they compare to alternatives. Various positioning strategies can be followed, such as those focused on specific product attributes, needs, benefits, user group (e.g., vegetarians), or against a primary (a direct competitor—Hilton and Marriott) or secondary competitor (Hilton and Holiday Inn).

The authors recommend a three-step positioning process: (1) identify possible competitive advantages to be used in positioning the business, (2) select what are thought to be the most suitable competitive advantages, and (3) "deliver" and "communicate" the selected position. Whatever the attribute or bundle of attributes, each firm must attempt to locate advantages that can help differentiate it from its major competitors. Examples include physical attributes, location, services offered, quality employees, and the overall image of the firm. Since it is not possible for every firm to develop significant competitive advantages, minor advantages must be sought. As the impact of a competitive advantage decreases, so does its longevity. For this reason, firms that focus on minor advantages may need to frequently change strategies to keep competitors off guard.

The determination of the right position should be based on the requirements of being important, distinctive, superior, communicable, preemptive, affordable, and profitable (Kotler et al., 1996, p. 264). After selecting the "positioning characteristics and a positioning statement," the business then determines how it will communicate the position and organize its marketing mix variables to support it.

ENDNOTES

[1] A destination is a firm, or group of firms, that attempts to attract consumers that live in other cities, states, regions, or countries.

[2] A simple method of creating a scale on a more easily understood, 100-point basis is to divide the derived score by the total possible score (e.g., 290 divided by 450 equals .58, then multiply this figure by 100 to yield a score of 58).

[3] Kotler distinguishing between *positioning*, which he sometimes terms product positioning, and *competitive position*. He does not use the term *market position*.

[4] Valid methodology allows researchers to be equally accurate in determining qualitative and quantitative attributes. For example, price is a quantitative measure; however, it has little meaning without associative qualitative measures that assess the customer's perception of it (i.e., high, low, good value, poor value, etc.).

[5] Other functional strategies (operational, financial, human resources, etc.) supportive of marketing mix variables should be required for a complete positioning strategy.

[6] It is questionable whether you separate positioning into objective and subjective components. Since we are dealing with perceptions, where does one draw the line? Is size, appearance, quantity, price, and so forth objective or subjective? It is probably of little or no value to separate tangible from intangible aspects of a firm's position. Later, the authors attempt to divide subjective into tangible and intangible components—an even more questionable concept. One valid point that they do bring up is the value of attempting to tangibilize the intangible.

[7] Saying that marketers should not be concerned if their image is true, as long as it is positive, is suggestive of manipulation or a lack of ethics. This situation, especially in the hospitality industry, where we have close contact with our guests and expose our facilities, is a short-term strategy. Perhaps Lewis et al. could have included more of an explanation.

⁸ According to Kendra Walker (1997, April 2) (Manager of Communications, Hilton Hotel Corporation, Beverly Hills, California), the "America's Business Address" campaign was one of the most successful in the history of Hilton. Where a normal campaign runs for about two years, this campaign ran for about ten years. It worked so well in differentiating Hilton as a business hotel that marketers had to develop mini-campaigns targeting different markets with non-business benefits. For example, since the hotel chain was known as the business address, weekend occupancy was not being maximized. In 1989, they developed the "Bounce Back Weekend" which took Saturday night from being the slowest night of the week to the second busiest of the week. Hilton also began acquiring resorts to position itself to non-business markets.

⁹ These are slogans or positioning slogans that may have been based on positioning statements. A positioning statement includes specific information that allows functional managers to create new strategies or to modify or discontinue existing strategies (see Chapter 4 for examples of positioning statements).

■ 4
The Positioning Process

POSITIONING is the junction point between business-level and functional-level strategic market planning. Business-level strategies help establish the target for positioning decisions—the customers/travelers to target and the basic product that will be offered (Reich, 1997a, 1997b). Subsequently, positioning is the process whereby management will decide how it wants these targeted travelers to view its destination relative to competing destinations. Functional-level strategies and tactics provide the specific actions that management will use to support the destination's desired position. (See Chapter 1 for a more thorough review of positioning's place in the planning process.)

For example, suppose that an increased focus on safety and security is a component of the destination's new business-level strategy. As the position of the destination is developed, it will focus on how the destination desires to be viewed from an overall standpoint (e.g., "An island with beautiful secluded beaches"), plus subordinate positioning concerning how it wants to be viewed regarding its performance on safety and security.

Later, in the development of functional strategies, various functional department heads would determine how they will deal with the safety and security issue. For example, operations might increase training, finance could approve new monitoring devices, and marketing could implicitly or explicitly include safety and security in promotions. Implicitly, phrases such as "leave your worries behind" or "the friendliest people in the world" can be included in slogans and supported with appropriate visual images. Explicitly, phrases such as, "One of the safest destinations in the world!" dealing directly with safety and security can be used.

Porter (1980, 1991), in an apparent attempt at clarifying the process, said that a suitable position is based on achieving a lower cost than competitors or the ability to differentiate one's offering and consequently command a premium price. While this is partially true, it is an overly simplistic view of strategy. Knowing that one should keep costs low and offer something different is simply the foundation of both financial and marketing success.

To effectively position a destination in the market, strategists need a process. While there is no process or formula that will yield a perfect positioning strategy, marketers must proceed in the most effective and efficient manner possible. The author, based on a substantial literature review plus over 30 years of experience, recommends the following process (see Figure 4.1): (1) determine the target customers' preferred combination of attributes, (2) locate the geographic destination's

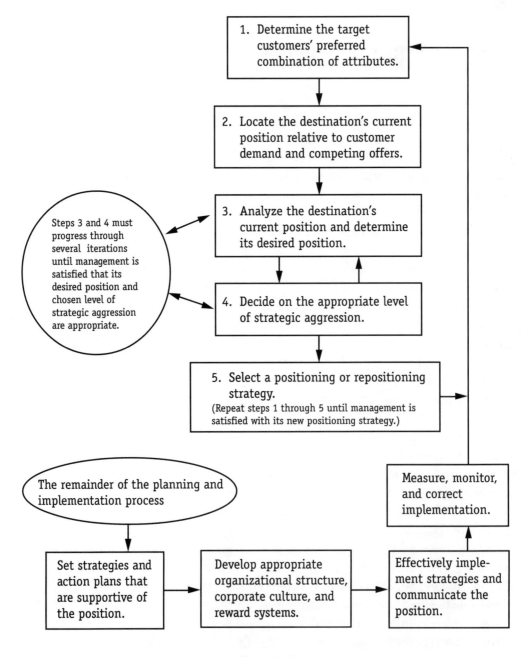

Figure 4.1:
The positioning process for tourism destinations

current position relative to customer demand and competing offers, (3) analyze the current position and determine the desired position, (4) decide on the appropriate level of strategic aggression change necessary to achieve the desired position), and (5) select a positioning or repositioning strategy. Each step will now be discussed in depth.

STEP #1. DETERMINE THE TARGET CUSTOMERS' PREFERRED COMBINATION OF ATTRIBUTES.

To develop a positioning strategy, marketers must have first systematically identified their target customer(s) and their demands and preferences (Barsky, 1992; Haahti, 1986; Martin, 1986a, 1986b; Swinyard & Struman, 1986). Personal review of many marketing plans shows that this is a commonly neglected area for potential sales increases. To varying degrees, many destination marketers will analyze their existing customer bases for unique characteristics, but may not take enough time to analyze the broader markets for untapped sources of customers (Talley, 1968). The reasons for this vary, but most common are the financial and career risks of focusing on new target groups and the fact that it is easier to repeat what has been done in the past.

The task of identifying preferred attributes is based on research methods (Luck & Rubin, 1987; Schiffman & Kanuk, 1991). Since the second step in the positioning process deals with locating a destination's position and concurrently has a major research component, readers can review it for recommendations on finding out what travelers expect. If desired, steps one and two of the positioning process can be combined. Researchers must use caution when attempting to derive an inordinate amount of information from respondents at one sitting. Additionally, asking respondents questions about general preferences, then following this with questions about how certain firms measure up to them may bias the results. For example, prior to being asked about their preferences, respondents have a certain image about their favorite destinations and how they would rank them. If respondents were asked in the same survey to express their preferences for various features of a destination, this thought process may cause them to question their cognitive hierarchy or positioning of the destinations. The remainder of this section will deal with maximizing this research effort.

Locating Small Gaps in Customer Information

If the customer characteristics identified are those that are commonly known and utilized in competitors' positioning strategies, then other factors must be sought that will allow the destination to stand out from competitors. Before the Medallion Hotel Corporation opened their first property under the Medallion name (formerly a Marriott in Houston, Texas), they surveyed their target markets to see what needs and wants were being satisfied and which were not. Among the many things learned was that after a long day of work, business people wanted to walk into a more relaxing lobby, not a monument to the hotel's designer. This resulted in a lobby that looks more like a contemporary upscale home, rather than a sensory overload of color and design. They also learned that customers were becoming de-sensitized to years of frequent guest programs and that they were also tired of waiting for benefits. The Medallion Hotels quite successfully took advantage of this situation by providing guests with gift certificates from Eddie Bauer clothing stores after a specified amount was spent at the hotel (about what would be spent for three nights at the hotel). While there was an initial drop in revenue after the name change, in less than one year occupancies were more than 10% higher than when the property was under the Marriott brand.

Magnifying Small Gaps

There are few physical differences between many of the Hilton and Marriott Hotels. They offer many of the same services, and generally are in close proximity to one another. In fact, some hotels, through changes in franchise contracts, may have been Hiltons or Marriotts that switched from one brand to the other. If their offerings are similar, management will have four key choices in their positioning decisions (Levitt, 1980). They could: (1) find out what services would be valued by the market that are not currently being offered (Getty & Thompson, 1994); (2) attempt to magnify irrelevant attributes (e.g., promoting Viennese desserts when target customers know nothing about Viennese desserts) (Carpenter, Glazer, & Nakamoto, 1994), (3) improve strategy implementation to a level that is obviously above that of primary competitors (Day & Wensley, 1988; Snow & Hrebiniak, 1980), or (4) focus on differentiating their properties through promotions (Porter, 1980). Promotions could attempt to magnify any minor differences between the two hotels, especially those related to various customer-demanded attributes. For example, Hilton Hotels positioned themselves away from "America's business address" to "So nice to come home to." The purpose was to capitalize on Hilton's reputation as the standard for the upper midscale market, while at the same time creating a more relaxing image than *a place for business.* The winner in the positioning battle between similar concepts will likely be the hotel that first locates the most meaningful tangible or intangible attributes, then packages and promotes them to the satisfaction of its target customers.

> The creation of the appropriate image will play a major role in determining which restaurant is positioned most effectively.

In some instances there may be noticeable differences in product strategies between primary competitors, such as between the Bennigan's and Friday's restaurants. When this occurs, management must find out what differences are most valued by its largest target customer groups, then attempt to highlight those differences in its positioning strategies, and communicate them through promotional strategies. Again, the creation of the appropriate image will play a major role in determining which restaurant is positioned most effectively.

Future Desired Attributes

As a destination tries to find that unique position in its market, it must obviously study its customers' preferences and competitors' offerings. But a critical component is the determination of what customers will desire in the near and long-term future. While this is not a simple task, it can often be determined by asking customers questions, such as "What do you not like about the current products and services we offer?" "How would you change our products and services to better make them meet your needs?" (questions similar to these could also be asked about primary or secondary competitor's offerings), "What are your favorite three geographic destinations/restaurants/hotels?" and "Do any of these come close to your ideal geographic destination/restaurant/hotel?" "Why?" and "Why not?" Finding out what customers like about current products is valuable, but in today's fast-changing market, this may not yield enough of a differentiation to locate a unique and defendable position.

Alternative Decision Makers

While it is important to monitor individual travelers' image of the destination, it is also essential for hotel management to monitor the opinions of decision makers who may never stay at the hotel. Meeting planners, travel planners, corporate secretaries, sales managers at various tourist bureaus, travel agents, and government officials will have vastly different objectives and desired attributes than individual customers. Rather than being primarily concerned with product, service quality, and price, monetary incentives and the decision maker's personal reputation may surface as key attributes.

User Status

In a survey with the purpose of finding out the objective position, it is best to ask groups with various levels of product usage and frequency. This allows management to expose potential problems with its image or positioning (Barich & Kotler, 1991). For example, non-users of the business's product or service may have a poor image of the business based on something that happened years ago. Low-frequency users may have somewhat different images of the business than high-frequency users. This information can be used to understand how these various interpretations influence the destination's overall market position.

STEP #2. LOCATE THE GEOGRAPHIC DESTINATION'S CURRENT LINEAR POSITION RELATIVE TO CUSTOMER DEMAND AND COMPETING OFFERS

Traditionally, the calculation of a destination's position requires a detailed analysis of all aspects of its internal activities (Bowles, 1991; Jeffrey & Hubbard, 1994) and its competitive marketplace (Cooper & Inoue, 1996; Hunt & Morgan, 1995; Kopalle & Lehmann, 1995; Purushottam & Krishnamurthi, 1996; Smith, Andrews, & Blevins, 1992). However, this process rarely attempts to locate the destination's current standing relative to customer demand and competing offers (Dodson, 1991; Kara, Kaynak, & Kucukemiroglu, 1995), a step that can help managers determine their relative market position in a similar manner to that used by consumers to perceptually rank competing offers (Reich, 1997b).

Market Position Model (Linear Positioning)

The market position model (Reich, 1997a, 1997b) (see Figure 4.2) is designed to (a) graphically display the destination and its environment, (b) help with the explanation and quantification of the destination's position relative to competing firms, and (c) assist in the selection of a future desired position. It is referred to as linear positioning because there is also a tendency for an organization's market position to move forward and backward in a linear manner. There is also generally a direct (linear) and graphable relationship between the image of a destination (and

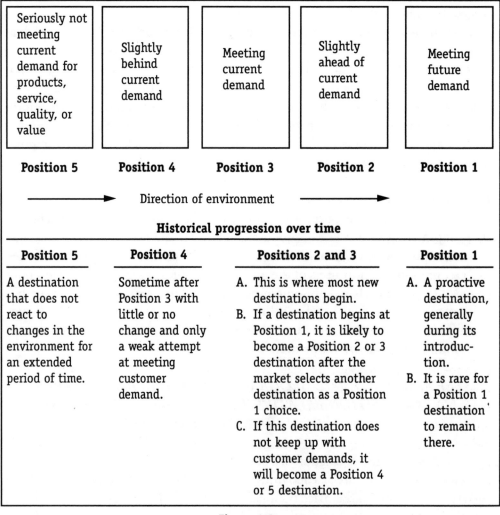

Figure 4.2:
Market position analysis for tourism destinations

the primary components of that image, such as product quality and value) and its financial success. The main advantage of the market position model over positioning maps is that it represents the overall or linear position, as opposed to its position on selected attributes. Since a destination's position could be made up of 40 or more individual attributes, positioning maps can only provide minimal assistance in determining the destination's overall position. Certainly, if desired, positioning maps can play a supportive role in this task, but they are more valuable and useful in determining the specifics of the future position, rather than determining the current overall position (examples of positioning maps will be described later in this section). The purpose here is not to discriminate between variables, but to position the destination based on how customers perceive it on a holistic basis. For example, if customers say they like competitor A more than competitor B, competitor A will occupy a better position than competitor B. Competitor B will be faced with the decision of the importance of attempting to change its current position. In addition to graphically showing the destination's position in the market, it also reveals the interaction between the environment and the competitive set of destinations in that environment.

Linear Competitive Comparison

This linear form of quantification allows for a comparison with competitors as a means of showing how well the market has received the geographic area's product offering. For example, knowing that a fierce competitor is one position ahead gives management rich information to help with strategic and tactical decisions. Management would analyze the reasons for the disparity in positions, then decide to remain in its current position or to narrow the gap through strategies similar to the competitor or by differentiation. It is important to stress that strategies would not be selected solely on the basis of relative positions. Sometimes a lesser position is all that a destination can reasonably expect. The destination's tourist traffic, revenues, and additional research information (the survey used to pinpoint the position) would serve as the primary justification for attempts at changing the destination's position. Management experience and intuition would also be considered.

Environmental Change

Another major purpose for the market position model is to show what happens to a destination's position over various periods of time, based on its strategized position, strategy selection, and the results of implementation. Since the environment is constantly moving, a destination that continues to offer the same products and promotions can only lose its current position in the market. There will always be exceptions, but as a general rule, customers' demands do not remain static. Some positions may be defendable for a decade or more. At some point though, customers' preferences change and competitors begin catering to those new demands. For example, Hawaii's market share of the tropical island tourist trade, though still satisfactory, is not what it was in the past.

The positions are categorized as follows:

Position 1.
This is a highly proactive or innovative destination that has found a major gap in the market, an unmet need sometimes referred to as meeting future demand—finding out what the customer will want in the future, then offering it now. Position 1 destinations will essentially create demand rather than follow the pack by meeting current demand. Position 1 generally includes only a small percentage of the geographic destinations for any market segment. Since this is a high-risk, high-return position, it may be tenuous, based on the strategies chosen, implementation, and sustainability. There is no simple means of finding out what it will take to reach Position 1, but theoretically what must be done is to find a gap between what is currently being offered and what customers want, then supplying it.

Few destinations have been able to remain at Position 1. Those with new and popular resorts will often achieve a Position 1 status because of the curiosity of target guests and their willingness to stay at the newest facility. However, as the newness wears off, the property and its location are soon viewed as a possible option, rather than one of the best options. Since one of the most popular reasons for traveling to any certain destination is for new and varied experiences, destinations must either offer something quite unique or attempt to have something for a variety of target markets.

In the short-term, proactive destinations do not necessarily have to remain proactive if they hope to continue their success, but they do need to be poised for change before the position is lost (Miller, 1994). For instance, a Position 1 destination could take an adaptive (moderate, selective change) or even passive (no change) strategic stance for several years, but at some point it would need to renew its proactive image to hold on to its Position 1 standing. There are a few destinations whose residents have exhibited extremely poor hospitality and remain high in travel preference. However, these are exceptions and nothing short of the Eiffel Tower, Arc de Triomphe, and a great bottle of Bordeaux could help duplicate their success.

> *In the short-term, proactive destinations do not necessarily have to remain proactive if they hope to continue their success, but they do need to be poised for change before the position is lost.*

Because of the greater degree of difficulty to change or upgrade concepts for destinations than for specific hospitality destinations, it is likewise more difficult for them to remain at Position 1. The vast majority of successful destinations are likely at Position 2—moderately innovative destinations that excel at implementing the basics on a consistent basis (McKee, Varadarajan, & Pride, 1989).

Position 2.

These locations are ahead of basic consumer demand, but not leaders in innovation. Some in Position 2 may never utilize innovation. Instead they will simply react to successful strategies of competitors (generally segment leaders), then focus on near flawless implementation to distinguish themselves. This position can be achieved in two ways. As difficult as it is for a destination to reach Position 1, it is probably more difficult to remain there. Few market players can continue hitting home runs, so as time passes Position 1 occupants will usually slip to Position 2. Risk-averse management and comfort with success are the two primary factors that cause this decline. To remain at Position 1, marketers must at some point develop new strategies, possibly not as innovative as those that brought them to Position 1, but exciting enough to gain the market's attention. Second, occasionally a Position 3 destination through radical or persistent changes and wide market acceptance will move forward to Position 2. This move will generally require extensive changes in all functional areas, especially effective promotions that saturate the destination's target market. Because of the difficulty of remaining at Position 1, the primary and realistic goal of most progressive destinations is to remain at Position 2. (It is rare for Position 4 or 5 destinations to attain Position 2 status.)

Position 3.

These destinations are meeting current demand with average quality and value. They may have begun here or slipped to this position by not keeping up with environmental changes. In some circumstances this position may in fact be quite advantageous. If customers are conservative and the destination has an established reputation, then meeting current demand could be just what customers expect. However, there normally comes a time when even the "We've been going there for years!" destination needs to make some changes. Position 3 occupants are in a comfort zone that can reap the benefits of stability. The chief problem, like that of Positions 1 and 2, is waiting too long to upgrade its offering and subsequently seeing its position decline. The Position 3 destination can best hold its position by waiting for trends to solidify before attempting to adopt them. If this destination ignores the need for incremental change and slips to Position 4, it may be quite difficult to reverse its downward trend.

Position 4.

This is a somewhat outdated destination. Position 4 occupants have not kept up with what customers are demanding or what competitors are offering. Frequently, destinations that have centered their tourism activities around a limited product offering end up here because of their product, rather than market focus. Hotel or restaurant destinations will rarely start out in Position 4 or 5. Those that do will generally not last for more than their working capital allows. The most common Position 4 destination is one that has been around for a long time with a small but relatively loyal customer base. As management became complacent, the destination gradually let its market standing slip to this position.

Tenure and Position Change

An important domain assumption for this model is that it will be possible to change a destination's position based on its tenure at its current position. For example, a destination that has been in Position 4 for several years before updating its product offering or promotional strategies will rarely move beyond Position 3. This is because there is a substantial brand image that must be overcome, making it difficult to convince its target market that it has gone from being a lesser option to being one of the best options. To move beyond Position 3, the destination would need to implement highly innovative strategies, most notably extensive renovations, new attractions, and saturate its target market and marketing intermediaries to make them aware of the changes. An effort of this magnitude is unlikely because of the unwillingness of management and owners to take the financial and career risks of attempting to rejuvenate an outdated or lackluster image.

Position 5.

This is a seriously outdated destination. A major turnaround strategy is necessary that will likely encompass all facets of the destination. Position 5 destinations, like those of Positions 3 and 4, will face a formidable challenge when attempting to improve their position. Rarely will any strategy allow a Position 5 destination to move immediately to Position 3 or higher without major changes. Because of their destination's poor image, local hospitality-related businesses are likely losing money, and perhaps are themselves at Position 4 or 5. Since few businesses have the reserves to linger at Position 5, they will likely be forced into deciding whether they should sell out or participate in cooperative promotions with their tourism bureau (or ad hoc organization formed to address the problem). Because of the expense involved and the probability that existing shareholders would be unwilling to accept the risk, poorly positioned firms in Position 5 destinations are often sold to firms in Position 1, 2, or 3 for repositioning, renovation, and rebranding.

Locating the Destination's and Competitors' Linear Positions

In the previous step, management found out what target markets think is important and other characteristics that will help improve the geographic area's competitive position. Now management must measure the degree to which its performance and the attractiveness of its geographic area has satisfied the demands of its target customers (Day & Wensley, 1988; Price, Arnould, & Tierney, 1995). Performance in this context will be expressed as the destination's *linear position,* relative to primary competitors.

Subjective vs. Objective Determination of Position

Management can either subjectively decide how the business is positioned or objectively query its customers to discover how they view the destination (Lapidus & Schibrowsky, 1994). Though the objectively determined position will be preferable in the vast majority of instances, subjective determination is preferable to ignoring the situation altogether. If adequate information is not available or if time is short, then the subjectively determined position may have to suffice. Since the customers of any one destination will also patronize other similar destinations, it is possible to accumulate adequate and relevant information about primary competitors through secondary sources, such as academic journals (Haywood, 1986).

Subjectively Determining the Destination's Position

The position can be based simply on management's opinion or determined by reviewing historical records, such as strategic or marketing plans. Its accuracy can be increased with quantitative support, such as the utilization of the unidimensional positioning scale, or with an analysis of the market by an unbiased third party with extensive industry experience. If these additional steps are not taken or are minimized, then whoever makes the assessment must attempt to be as realistic as possible. For a subjective assessment of the destination's position, management should analyze: (1) changes in sales or visitation patterns from year to year; (2) changes in competing destinations' sales or visitation patterns from year to year; (3) whether competitors have ceased offering products that are similar to one's offering; (4) if competitors with similar target customers are outperforming one's destination with an updated or innovative concept, or new product; (5) if traffic counts for the destination are decreasing; (6) whether the local area appears dated; and (7) if customers have been commenting or complaining about strategic factors.

Objectively Determining the Destination's Position

The position can be determined informally by interviews, or ideally, formally by surveys. Much can be learned by asking a reasonable number of customers about their perception of the destination—what do they think of when the geographic location is mentioned (Callan, 1994, 1995)?

The business's choice of the type and number of questions to ask and scaling (response) formats should be based on management's knowledge of research and statistical theory. There is no need in asking 40 questions if the results cannot be effectively tabulated and interpreted. If there is no one inside the destination with these skills, then questions should be held to a minimum or the hiring of an outside marketing consultant should be considered. The critical point is that effective consumer research can vastly improve the business's knowledge of its target customers, its performance in meeting their needs, and therefore its ability to identify the most viable present and future opportunities (Priceet al., 1995; Tse, 1988).

Multidimensional Measurement

Though a unidimensional positioning scale can be used, a multidimensional positioning scale will allow researchers to uncover specific perceptions of targeted travelers (Davis & Cosenza, 1988; Hair, Anderson, Tatham, & Black, 1995)—perceptions that can be used later to identify, understand, and predict specific behaviors (e.g., those related to transportation costs; lodging quality; and supportive attractions, such as museums, national parks, and so forth); to more fully understand the destination's relative position; and subsequently in the creation of a positioning statement (step number five of the positioning process).

Unidimensional Positioning Scales

Since the primary questions in any research effort are the validity and reliability of the data, occasionally a unidimensional scale will suffice. Figure 4.3 provides a unidimensional Likert-type interval scale (intervally scaled ordinal measurement) that according to Kerlinger (1973) can be used to obtain a mean (average) ranking for applicable destinations. It would be beneficial to obtain further demographic, psychographic, and behavioral data for analysis. If utility and cost are the primary reasons for proceeding with a unidimensional scale, the need for additional supportive data may preclude this choice. That is, if you will be gathering additional data anyway, perhaps a multidimensional scale will require little extra effort.

One of the first questions regarding measurement scales is if those already tested by other researchers can be used or if a specific scale must be developed. The most expeditious path would be the utilization of existing scales that have be shown

---

- Please rank your image of the destinations below according to the five position categories that follow. Your image is simply how you feel about the destination, whether you have been there or not (an item noting whether the respondent has visited the destination would prove additional understanding). It is okay to rate more than one destination for any specific position. For example, if you felt inclined, you could designate two destinations as a Position 1, four destinations as a Position 3, two Position 4, and so forth.

- Please read the Position category requirements carefully.

Position 1:   should greatly exceed guests' expectations
Position 2:   should exceed guests' expectations
Position 3:   should meet guests' expectations
Position 4:   may not meet guests' expectations
Position 5:   will likely not meet guests' expectations

A. St. Martin   C. Bermuda   E. Bahamas   G. Puerto Rico
B. Aruba   D. Jamaica   F. St. Thomas H. Florida Keys

- Place the letter of the destination in what you feel is the appropriate position category.

Position 1 ____ ____ ____ ____ ____ ____ ____ ____
Position 2 ____ ____ ____ ____ ____ ____ ____ ____
Position 3 ____ ____ ____ ____ ____ ____ ____ ____
Position 4 ____ ____ ____ ____ ____ ____ ____ ____
Position 5 ____ ____ ____ ____ ____ ____ ____ ____

Figure 4.3:
Unidimensional positioning measurement

to be valid in measuring the constructs of interest across different populations (known as an etic instrument). In unique situations, there may be previous (secondary) research whose situation so closely parallels one's own that the results can be effectively utilized. The problem with these strategies is that even though the same attributes may appear appropriate for different situations or geographic locations, the lack of an attempt at identifying key, situation-specific attributes may cloud the study's applicability. Subsequently, the assumed etic instrument (applicable to different contexts) may not be appropriate. To reduce the possibility of having an invalid scale, an emic instrument (also referred to as interpretivist, contextual, or situation specific) can be developed. Emic scales are normally developed based on a combination of the marketer's experience, available secondary information, and some type of primary research.

In some cases, researchers will already have an internal and valid database of travelers' opinions of key attributes of both the destination and its primary competitors. This database could be from recent formal surveys or, if randomly distributed, comment cards. If it is felt that this database is current and suitable for determining the destination's strategized position, then it can be used to determine the linear position. If not, marketers must decide whether to re-implement the past survey instrument, prepare a new instrument, or to use a separate unidimensional scale as previously discussed.

The Three-Horned Dilemma

In a modern technologically based society, availability and gathering of data is not a major problem. The most difficult question for researchers is to determine which source or type of data should be relied upon. Can researchers rely on secondary research from academic journals or various governmental tourism agencies? Or would they be better off utilizing a primary research strategy, such as through survey or experiments? This question, or, as McGrath et al. (1982) termed it, *the three-horned dilemma,* must be confronted (also see Runkel & McGrath, 1972). The three horns of the dilemma are generalizability, precision, and context. The concept is that if a research method that yields one type of data is chosen, then the other two horns of the dilemma are sacrificed.

For example, a research approach that focuses on interviews at the marketer's destination should provide accurate contextual data. However, the ability of marketers to generalize to the population or to expect precision may be limited.

The simplest solution to the dilemma would be to utilize a broad-based research strategy. The problem with this decision is that as more methods of research are utilized, the cost and time necessary to gather the data increase. Generally, the most effective and efficient solution is to utilize some reasonable combination of research methods. Because of the volume of available high-quality and generalizable secondary research for tourism, the solution is relatively simple. Utilize these sources along with minimal primary research.

Variable Selection

In the context of variables for destination positioning research, the following variables/topics could be considered, along with those in Figure 4.4, and the lists of typical variables from prior tourism research. Focus groups could also be utilized to gather more contextual items (Churchill, 1979). An advantage of focus groups for the development of a questionnaire is that the targeted sample/respondents will find the wording of the instrument to "be familiar, meaningful, and unambiguous" (Sheth et al., 1991, p. 93).

- Desired attributes in geographic destinations (e.g., transportation, lodging, and dining costs; quality issues related to these three dimensions; physical features that travelers expect from the destination, such as mountains, oceans/seas, snow, beaches, historical attractions, sight-seeing, shopping areas, and sports/recreation facilities; intangibles that travelers expect from the destination, such as excitement/risk, novelty, socializing, education, and being able to tell friends about great trip)
- Desired attributes in hotels (e.g., cost of rooms; quality of rooms; cleanliness of rooms; atmospherics (design/decor); efficiency and courtesy of employees; location being near attractions; food if available; and safety and security issues)
- Desired attributes in restaurants (e.g., cost of food and beverages; quality of food and beverages; cleanliness and sanitation; efficiency and courtesy of employees; and location attributes)
- Demographic variables
- Consumption characteristics, such as non-users, low-, medium-, or high-frequency users.

Typical Variables in Tourism Research

The following studies include common variables that can help guide researchers' efforts. As previously discussed, the variables for destination positioning should be specifically developed for each study. However, relatively recent data may be suitable if there have been only minor changes in the market. If there are highly similar destinations that are direct competitors, and if this data is available, it may also be appropriate. The studies are in alphabetical order of their authors.

Dann (1995)

Domain: Geographic Destinations

Primary construct: Destination image based on socio-linguistic perceptions (verbal responses to sociologically oriented pictures)

This research allowed respondents to identify their own variables/dimensions (open ended), rather than providing a static, closed-ended questionnaire. Respondents were asked for their cognitive, affective, and conative images of Barbados in four different situations: (1) pre-trip holistic impression, (2) pre-trip impression of a picture from a Barbados Board of Tourism brochure, (3) on-trip holistic impres-

Products/Services
Quality
Consistency
Selection (menu and service mix)
Speed of service
Interior atmosphere
Exterior atmosphere
Cleanliness
Reservations
Safety/security
Convenient operating hours

Supportive Attractions
Events, festivals, etc.
Tours
Theme parks
National parks
Museums
Historical landmarks/sites
Nightlife
Shopping
Restaurants
Hotels

Price
Value
Fairness relative to competition
Price range

Location/Infrastructure
Convenient location(s)
Access (ingress/egress)
Parking
Roads
Transportation
Mountains
Recreational water
    (rivers, oceans, etc.)

Promotions
Merchandising
Advertising
Public relations
Sales promotions
Message
    Consistent
    Memorable
    Effective
    Influenced purchase decision

Psychological/Personal Factors
(Used primarily in tourism research)
Crowdedness
Economic development
Extent of commercialism
Personal safety
Degree of urbanization
Friendliness of residents
Adventure
Educational/cultural
Reputation
Political stability

Corporate Philosophies,
    Practices, and Traits
Charitable donations
Community involvement
Responsible member of community
Ecological impact and recycling
    efforts
Reputation as a quality employer
Reputation for quality in all facets
    of business
Reputation of management
Goals of ownership
Goals of management
Aggressiveness of decision makers

Human Resources
Conscientious/empathy
Dependable
Appearance
Manners
Hygiene

Sales Staff
Professionalism
Courtesy
Efficiency/responsiveness
Dependability
Knowledge
Ethics/honesty
Empathy/responsiveness
Support during functions
Anticipates needs
Billing accuracy

**Figure 4.4: Common variables in destination positioning research
(including geographic, hotels, and restaurant destinations)**

sion, and (4) on-trip impression of a picture from a Barbados Board of Tourism brochure. They were then asked for their impressions. The concepts behind this research method were the realization that individuals' motivations and actions may have little to do with inherent dimensions of the destination, that items may have different meanings to different respondents, and that validity is too often sacrificed in promotion of expediency.

Variables: (In each of the cases below, the picture provided was that of a young couple on a beach at sunset.)

Cognitive Pre-trip: A tropical island like Martinique or St. Lucia

- *On-trip:* It's a tropical island, but not really like Martinque or St. Lucia. In the countryside there are some similarities, but Barbados is very flat. The people drive on the wrong side of the road.
- *Pre-trip with picture:* Reminds me of Hawaii—a romantic getaway.
- *On-trip with picture:* I haven't seen a sunset yet. It's always been cloudy. There are palm trees.

Affective Pre-trip: A very relaxing place to come. A low-key place to unwind with warm weather.

- *On-trip:* Very friendly people; clean and safe. More secure than other places. Safer than home.
- *Pre-trip with pictures:* A lover's paradise. You can leave your worries behind.
- *On-trip with pictures:* It is not a lover's paradise. I have not seen any secret beaches like this one here.

Conative Pre-trip: Scenery is absolutely beautiful—palm trees, beaches. That's what I vision in my head: water-skiing, friendly people, being on the beach—the beach with my wife—that's what I envision.

- *On-trip:* It's everything I imagined, everything and better. It's total relaxation, a different world away from the hustle and bustle. Isolated from the world as far as the United States is concerned. I like the laid-back attitude of the people toward life.
- *Pre-trip with picture:* My wife and I on the beach enjoying our 25th anniversary.
- *On-trip with picture:* Paradise. My wife and I on the beach enjoying our 25th anniversary. As beautiful as the picture.

Echtner and Ritchie (1993)

Domain: Geographic Destinations

Primary construct: Destination image based on functional and psychological attributes

Variables: Functional attributes: Tourist sites/activities, national parks/wilderness activities, historic sites/museums, beaches, fairs (exhibits and festivals), scenery/natural attractions, nightlife and entertainment, shopping facilities, facilities for information and tours, sports facilities/activities, local infrastructure/transportation, cities, accommodations, restaurants, architecture, cost/price levels, climate.

Psychological attributes: Crowdedness, cleanliness, degree of urbanization, economic development/affluence, extent of commercialization, political stability, accessibility, personal safety, ease of communication, customs/culture, different cuisine/food and drink/hospitality/friendliness/receptiveness, restful/relaxing, atmosphere (familiar versus exotic), opportunity for adventure, opportunity to increase knowledge, family or adult oriented, quality of service, fame/reputation.

Embacher and Buttle (1989)

Domain: Summer Vacation/Geographic Destination

Primary construct: Image

Variables: Genuine culture/artificial "tourist" culture, tourism very organized/less organized, reliable weather/unreliable weather, cheap/expensive, boring destination/interesting destination, and beautiful countryside/built-up, man-made environment.

Filiatrault and Ritchie (1988)

Domain: Table-Service Restaurants

Primary constructs: Situational factors, product offering

Variables: Situational variables: "Weekday lunch with associates and/or friends with individuals paying their own bill, an important business dinner with a prestigious guest with expenses paid from company funds, an evening weekend meal with spouse and two children under 12 years of age; it is a family tradition to dine out in this fashion approximately once a month" (p. 31), *Product offering:* type of cuisine (European, Asiatic, specialty, North American), price (up to $4.99 per person, $5.00 to $11.99 per person, $12 and above per person), quality of service (prestigious and elaborate, simple and courteous), ambiance (cozy and pleasant, lively and busy), and quality of food (always excellent, good).

Madrigal and Kahle (1994)

Domain: Vacation Activities/Geographic Destination

Primary constructs: Personal values and vacation activity preferences

Variables: Personal values: From factor analysis, personal values were reduced to four factors—external (being well respected, sense of belonging, and security), enjoyment/excitement (fun and enjoyment, and excitement), achievement (accomplishment, self-fulfillment), and egocentrism (self-respect and warm relationships with others). These are the same nine values used in Muller (1991). *Vacation preferences:* Four factors and their underlying variables—culture (visit historic sites, visit scenic sites, visit museums, learn about local culture), outdoor (camping, hiking/backpacking, hunting/fishing), exercise (jogging, aerobics, tennis), and roots (visit ancestral homelands, visit friends and/or relatives).

Mazanec (1995)

Domain: Luxury Hotel Attributes

Primary construct: Position/image

Variables: Modern, expensive, exclusive, classical, relaxing, loud, romantic, old, friendly people, international, comfortable, clean, traditional, cold, picturesque, out of the ordinary, imaginative, formal, elegant, fun, noisy, contemplative, cozy, entertaining, intimate, boring, artificial, plain, value for money, obtrusive, unique, and atmospherics.

Moutinho (1987)

Domain: Conceptualization of Consumer Behavior Tourism

Primary constructs: Motivation, perceptions, attitudes, beliefs, personality/self-image, social image

Variables: Individual variables: Educational and cultural (to see how people in other countries live and work; to see particular sights, monuments or works of art; to gain a better understanding of current events; to attend special cultural or artistic events), relaxation, adventure and pleasure (to get away from everyday routine and obligations; to see new places, people, or seek new experiences; to have a good time, fun; to have some sort of romantic (sexual) experience, health and recreation (to rest and recover from work and strain; to practice sports and exercise), ethnic and family (to visit places your family came from; to visit relatives and friends; to spend time with the family and children), social and competitive (to be able to talk about places visited; because it is fashionable; to show that one can afford it). *Family variables:* type of lodging accommodation, vacation destination(s), children, length of vacation, transportation, activities, dollars spent.

Muller (1991)

Domain: International Tourists

Primary construct: Personal values, touristic attractiveness of a large city

Variables: Personal values: Self-respect, security, warm relationships with others, a sense of accomplishment, fun and enjoyment in life, self-fulfillment, being well respected, a sense of belonging, excitement (based on Rokeach's 1973 reduction of his original 18-item values scale). *Touristic attractiveness:* Safety from crime during your visit, hotel accommodation meeting your standards, being in a clean and well-kept city, ease of finding/reaching places of interest, availability of good health care in emergencies, friendliness and helpfulness of citizens, seeing a city with great scenic beauty, attractiveness of price levels, large choice of good restaurants, pleasantness of city's weather during visit, avoiding the feeling of being a stranger, experiencing artistic/cultural offerings, shopping in stores during visit, avoiding crowds and congestion, and experiencing city's nightlife/entertainment.

Reilly (1990)

Domain: Tourism in Montana

Primary construct: Image

Variables: (Variables were based on free elicitation, rather than forcing responses to a existing scale.) Pretty/scenic/beautiful, big/desolate/open/barren, mountains/big mountains, cold/bad weather, big sky/blue sky, wooded/forest/trees, remote/

rural/few people, western/cowboys/Indians, plains/flat/prairies, friendly people, fishing/good fishing, and skiing/good skiing.

Snepenger and Milner (1990)
Domain: Business Travelers

Primary constructs: Demographics, behaviors (pre-trip, on-location, and post-trip)

Variables: Sex, age, occupation, education, marital status, income, travel agent, previous visitation, business activity, and trip purpose (whether combined business and pleasure, or business only).

Data Presentation
After the information is gathered it may be necessary to further sub-divide or organize it to allow for a closer appraisal or prioritization. A matrix analysis of the most promising traveler segments is a common option. Figure 4.5 represents the segmentation variables for an island hotel. Possible categories for analysis would include individual business travelers (IBTs), corporate business, and leisure travelers. Along with associations, IBTs would likely be a secondary target market.

Multidimensional Positioning Scales for Various Forms of Analysis
The attitude of image can be measured in a variety of ways. Typically, it is based solely on cognitive (evaluative/rational) perceptions/responses or through measuring both cognitive and affective (feeling/emotional) perceptions/responses for each scale item (as in the Fishbein & Ajzen-type models in Chapter 2). Seminal theorists have observed that cognitive and affective perceptions are closely linked (Rokeach, 1968) and that affect dominates the relationship (Sherif et al., 1965). While cognitive responses may not weigh as heavily in determining behavior as affect, it is an extremely valuable variable in measuring perception of the object of interest. Examples of each of these types of questions follow:

Cognitive:

The cost of travel to France is:

1. Very low;   2. Low;   3. Average;
4. Somewhat high;   5. Very high

Cognitive Affective:
(The above cognitive response would be multiplied by the following affective response.)

I feel the cost of air fare to Florida:

1. Is low enough so that it would not be a consideration in my decision to travel there;
2. Would be a minor consideration in my decision to travel there;
3. Would be a moderate consideration in my decision to travel there:
4. Would be a major consideration in my decision to travel there;
5. Would keep me from traveling there.

Cognitive responses can be used in several different ways. Typical methods include: (1) using individual responses for correlations and various forms of univariate and multivariate statistics (e.g., comparing cost of the trip to destination preference); (2) a new variable can be created by summing the responses (total cognitive

Segmentation Characteristic	Individual Business Travel (IBT)	Corporate Group	Leisure
Geographics Primary cities or countries of origin	U.S. (New York, San Francisco, Chicago) Canada Japan	U.S. (Dallas, Houston, Phoenix, Los Angeles) Germany Hong Kong	U.S. (Miami, New York, San Diego) Japan Taiwan
Demographics Household income	$75K	$83K	$88K
Education	10% high school 15% some college 75% college	20% high school 30% some college 50% college	10% high school 20% some college 70% college
Family cycle	Singles, families with one or two children	Singles, families without children	35- to 45-year-old singles and married couples
Psychographics Political orientation	Liberal to moderate	Liberal to moderate	Moderate to conservative
Sports orientation	Some active, some sedentary	Moderately active	Active to moderately active
Buyer Behavior Percentage of guests	5 percent	55 percent	23 percent
Price sensitivity	Low	Moderate to high	Moderate
Frequency of travel	12 times per year	2 times per year	Once per year
Brand loyalty	High	Medium to low	Medium
Product/service quality orientation	High	Medium	High
Principal benefits sought	Consistency, business services, technology	Consistency, price, meeting rooms, personalized service	Cleanliness, safety and security, excitement/variety

Figure 4.5:
Segmentation characteristics for the Oceanview Inn

perceptions); and (3) similarly, the sum could be divided by the number of items (questions) in the scale. If the scale is based on both cognitive and affective perceptions, then each pair of responses would be multiplied (referred to as a multiplicative variable). At this point there are two options: (1) the sum of their products would become a new variable (Lutz, 1977) (referred to as an *index of cognitive structure*, $\sum B_i a_i$); and (2) the sum of the products could be divided by the number of items in the scale. These new variables could then be used as a metric variable for various statistical analyses.

Calculating the Linear Position Using a Single-Construct Multidimensional Scale

While management will find valuable information from the analysis of means and frequencies (descriptive statistics) and higher order statistics (inferential statistics), it is imperative that an overall score be established for the destination. When using a multidimensional scale for measuring a destination's linear position, it can simply be a summated scale that is then divided by the number of items in the scale (e.g., 2.3 + 3.4 + 3.1 + 2.7 + 3.3 = 14.8; 14.8 ÷ 5 = 3; rounded from 2.96). This individual score for each destination becomes its linear position. Performance scores for various categories of questions within the composite score, such as questions about transportation costs, lodging, or food quality can be totaled or analyzed separately to provide functional departments with more specific assessment information.

The following is an example of the above described scale and calculations:

Marketing Questionnaire

The following questions are for the purpose of determining your perception of certain destinations. This survey should take about 5 minutes or less to complete. We appreciate your help. This information will help provide future visitors with an improved travel experience.

Thank you,
Gabriel Yukon, Marketing Manager

Geographic Destinations

Variables were selected from Muller (1991).
1. Hotel accommodation meeting your standards
2. Large choice of good restaurants
3. Attractiveness of price levels
4. Being in a clean and well-kept city
5. Safety from crime during your visit
6. Availability of good health care in emergencies
7. Seeing a city with great scenic beauty
8. Friendliness and helpfulness of citizens
9. Experiencing artistic/cultural offerings
10. Shopping in stores during visit

A. St. Martin   C. Bermuda   E. Bahamas   G. Puerto Rico
B. Aruba   D. Jamaica   F. St. Thomas   H. Florida Keys

Please read the Position category requirements carefully.
Position 1: should greatly exceed guests' expectations
Position 2: should exceed guests' expectations
Position 3: should meet guests' expectations
Position 4: may not meet guests' expectations
Position 5: will likely not meet guests' expectations

1. Did hotel accommodation meeting your standards?
Place the letter of the destination in what you feel is the appropriate Position category.

Example (All responses here are hypothetical/contrived.)
Position 1 __A__ __E__ ____ ____ ____ ____ ____ ____
Position 2 __D__ ____ ____ ____ ____ ____ ____ ____
Position 3 __C__ __B__ ____ ____ ____ ____ ____ ____
Position 4 __H__ __G__ ____ ____ ____ ____ ____ ____
Position 5 __F__ ____ ____ ____ ____ ____ ____ ____

Calculation of the Mean for an Ordinal Scale

The calculations for each item in the scale would be the same as that for the unidimensional measurement previously described.

Puerto Rico: 1 _35_   2 _21_   3 _24_   4 _12_   5 _9_
Category times the category responses (e.g., 2 x 21 = 42):

35	42	72	48	45

Sum of products for question #1: 242
Mean for question #1: 2.4 (242 ÷ 101 = 2.4; rounded from 2.39)
Means for questions 2 through 10: #2 - 1.3; #3 - 2.5; #4 - 2.1; #5 - 1.4; #6 - 2.3; #7 - 1.6; #8 - 1.8; #9 - 1.9; #10 - 2.7.
Total of mean responses: 20.0
The linear position (grand mean) for Puerto Rico would then be 2.0 (20.0 ÷ 10 = 2.0). The same process would be completed for each destination (geographic, hotel, restaurant, resort, etc.).

Linear Position Using a Two-Construct Multidimensional Scale

If it is decided that additional information regarding individuals' preferences is beneficial, a two-variable attitude scale can be used. The two variables are simply added, then divided by 2. Though this methodology differs from typical two-variable multiplicative attitude scales, it results in a number that can be used for a five-point positioning scale. For example, if the cognitive (evaluative/rational) and affective (feeling/emotional) scores were 2.4 and 3.1 respectively, the variable's index would be 2.8 (rounded from 2.75). The index for each set of variables would then be added and divided by the number of pairs of variables in the scale. The following example is for a five-item scale:

		Cognitive	Affective	Sum	Average
Question	#1	1.2	1.4	2.6	1.3
	#2	1.4	1.7	3.1	1.6
	#3	1.8	1.9	3.7	1.9
	#4	1.9	2.3	3.2	1.6
	#5	2.1	2.4	4.5	2.3
				Total	8.7
				Grand Mean	1.7

STEP #3. ANALYZE THE GEOGRAPHIC DESTINATION'S CURRENT POSITION AND DETERMINE ITS DESIRED POSITION

Each position is based on past strategic decisions and the degree of success with which they were implemented. It is important that management objectively determine why the destination is in its current position. A destination's market position will be based on the totality of the efforts of each functional department. Prior to functional decisions and action, the marketing department or its strategic counterpart, strategic marketing management (or strategic management) will determine broadly how the destination will compete—the products to be offered and the markets to target. Once this decision is made, it is the responsibility of each functional department within a destination to develop strategies and tactics that will help the destination maximize its market position. For example, the first functional responsibility lies with the marketing department. They will determine the most effective combination of products (goods and services) to offer, pricing structures, and develop a proposed promotional plan. Even though the human resources department is not directly responsible for achieving marketing objectives, the employees it hires will be. Therefore, each employee hired must exemplify the desired image of the destination. Various operational components of the destination will likewise be responsible for creation and delivery of the product. Finally, these functional strategies and tactics will be implemented. Their success, along with the impact of environmental factors such as competitors' actions, the economy, and societal changes, will determine the destination's market position.

A geographic destination must determine its desired position, because this will tell all within the organization (destination or responsible association for a geographic location) where it wants to be and how resources should be allocated. Question #4 will ask management to decide how aggressive it must be to achieve the desired position.

Market Position/Profit Model

Figure 4.6 is a market position model that adds the concept of profit to the analysis. Profit, in reference to geographic destinations, can be considered the overall profit of tourism-related entities, relative to competing geographic destinations. The reason for this addition is that a destination may be in one position but producing the profit of destinations in other positions. For example, a Position 3 destination that is producing the profit of a Position 1 or 2 destination (Position 3,2 or 3,1 in Figure 4.6) may decide that it is best to continue with existing strategies rather than risk change. Conversely, a Position 3 destination with the profit of a Position 4 or 5 destination (Position 3,4 or 3,5) might decide that its market position is okay, but either costs must be reined in or sales must be increased. If cost reduction was not the most effective remedy, then strategies targeted at increasing sales and probably its position should be considered.

There have been instances where destinations were extremely proactive but, for one reason or another, were not realizing the benefits of their position. The most frequent reasons for this have been financial problems, such as a massive debt, a large corporate overhead, or ineffective financial or accounting control systems. There may also be management or marketing problems, such as maintenance or repair problems with capital assets, inefficient operations, an entrenched bureaucracy, or many poor locations, or possibly the market that has enthusiastically accepted the product or service is too small to allow for a reasonable profit.

STEP #4. DECIDE ON THE APPROPRIATE LEVEL OF STRATEGIC AGGRESSION

Once management has located the destination's current position, it will then be faced with the task of deciding on the appropriate level of strategic aggression (level of change) necessary to move toward its desired position. Since at some point the majority of existing strategies will need to be changed, management should not be too pensive when hanging on to old habits (Mayersohn, 1994). Destinations that lack at least a moderate degree of uniqueness when compared to competitors will invariably be positioned behind them. The choices are (a) proactive, (b) reactive, (c) passive, (d) adaptive, and (e) discordant (not a viable selection, one that is acquired, rather than chosen) (see Figure 4.7).

Proactive

Being *proactive* can be defined as accessing future opportunities and threats, deciding which could provide avenues or hindrances to growth and profit, then acting on the assessment before competitors. A proactive stance can come from the development of an entirely new or innovative strategy (Drucker, 1985; Ross, 1985), capitalizing on an existing trend by incorporating more of its elements into the business than competitors (Quinn, 1985), seeking incremental innovation through improvements in existing practices (Brown, 1991; Stalk, Evans, & Shulman, 1992), or reviving a strategy from the past. Normally, being proactive is associated with the

Market Position Ranking (Relative to primary competitors)

1=Recognized as a leader in the industry, highly proactive, exceeding customer demand, top 5% of firms in market segment

2=Somewhat proactive, ahead of basic customer demand, upper 80% to 95% of firms

3=Generally reacts to strategic moves of other firms, meeting basic customer demands and expectations, middle 30% to 80% of firms

4=Not quite meeting customer demands or expectations, lower 10% to 30% of firms

5=Far behind current customer demand, marketing strategies are very outdated and execution is not meeting customer expectations, lower 10% of firms

Profit Position Ranking (Relative to primary competitors)

1=Upper 10% of industry range
2=Upper 65% to 90% of industry range
3=Middle 35% to 65% of industry range
4=Lower 15% to 35% of industry range
5=Bottom 15% of industry range

General Directions
1. As objectively as possible, rank your firm and a reasonable number of primary competitors.
2. Justify and record the reasons for how you positioned your firm and competitors.
3. Change management
A. Does your position need improvement?
B. What is your desired position?
C. What are the necessary resources and risks associated with this desired position?

Direction of Environment/Market

Market Position

Profit Position	1- Far exceeds current customer demand	2- Ahead of current customer demand	3- Meeting current customer demand	4- Slightly behind current customer demand	5- Far behind customer demand (outdated)
1- High	1,1	2,1	3,1	4,1	5,1
2- Above Average	1,2	2,2	3,2	4,2	5,2
3- Average	1,3	2,3	3,3	4,3	5,3
4- Below Average	1,4	2,4	3,4	4,4	5,4
5- Low	1,5	2,5	3,5	4,5	5,5

Figure 4.6: Market position/profit matrix

future. The key yardstick of proactiveness is actually being first. By the time Hyatt Hotels implemented their strategy of offering rooms with a wide array of business services, all of these services had been available for many years. They were simply the first to promote them as a package.

In the ideal case early innovators will accrue advantages of increased sales, profit, and improvements in image that can lead to sustainable competitive advantages (Makridakis, 1991). Hawaii, the first major island retreat; Hilton, the first major upper-midscale hotel property; Holiday Inn, the first major midpriced hotel chain; Motel 6, the first major budget hotel chain, attest to the fact that being first with something desired, but not currently offered, can be quite beneficial.

Important to the selection of proactive strategies is the destination's ability to carry out the strategies (Covin, 1991; Feltenstein, 1986). The need for an accurate

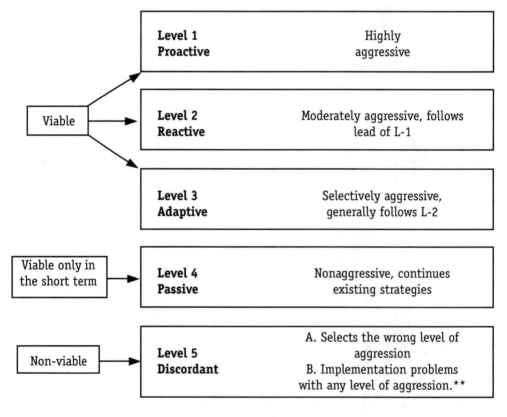

Figure 4.7:
Levels of strategic aggression*

* The higher the degree of strategic aggression, the higher the potential reward, and concurrently, the higher the potential for negative results. (See ** for a further explanation.)

** The degree of discord accompanying poor implementation is directly related to the level of strategic aggression. Poorly implemented level 1 strategies (proactive strategies) will have the highest degree of discord—the highest risk of negative results. Poorly implemented passive strategies (continuance of existing strategies) have the lowest degree of discord—generally, the lowest risk of negative results. In other words, the larger the mistake, the higher the discord.

assessment of the destination's ability increases with the degree of risk involved. Also critical to the proactiveness decision are the cross-functional cooperation of the destination's different functional departments and the timing and aggressiveness of the new product announcement. Empirical research by Olson, Walker, and Ruekert (1995) showed that highly innovative strategies are best implemented by cross-functional teams, where less innovative strategies, such as product improvements, are more effectively directed by the individual functional department closest to the product's production. New product announcements (NPAs) obviously serve the purpose of informing customers with the ultimate objective being to increase sales. However, they also let competitors know about the introduction. There are two options to decreasing or reducing competitor reaction. One is to keep the introduction secret until the new product is available for purchase. If this is a new location, secrecy may be a problem. If it is a major menu introduction, then this strategy may be a reasonable option. The second option for NPAs is to limit the aggressiveness with which the announcement is made. An announcement that proposes a major change in product offerings or one that is heavily focused on comparisons will often bring a quicker and stronger response from primary competitors (Green, Barclay, & Ryans, 1995; Robertson, Eliashberg, & Rymon, 1995).

A key to earning the designation of being a proactive destination is the speed with which a new product is brought to market. Time lapses can dilute potential impact, allowing competitors to either catch up or beat the destination to market. A study by Arthur D. Little (cited in Topfer, 1995) shows that increases in research and development costs associated with speeding product introduction resulted in only minimal reductions in revenue as compared to delays in introduction.

One of the reasons that entrepreneurial destinations frequently outperform conservative destinations is because of an increased propensity toward risk. They are usually smaller, less bureaucratic, and in need of strategies that help differentiate themselves from larger competitors. This allows the entrepreneurial destination to take a more proactive stance when it comes to taking advantage of potential opportunities. Conservative destinations, on the other hand, tend to be risk-averse, non-innovative, and reactive (Covin, 1991).

The quicker any organization can identify and begin posturing toward an opportunity-producing trend, the greater its lead time, the stronger its applicable skills, and therefore, the greater its competitive advantage over rivals.

Reactive

Probably the largest number of geographic destinations choose to adopt a reactive posture. This is reacting to or pursuing others' viable proactive strategies. The primary benefits of being reactive are that strategic mistakes are generally minimized and there is an above average degree of stability. For example, revenue for reactors are generally stable, as are management tenure, tourism bureau performance, and customer loyalty. The problem is that because of being just a little late in recognizing the trend, the destination's full potential was not realized. The quicker any organization can identify and begin posturing toward an opportunity-producing trend, the greater its lead time, the stronger its applicable skills, and therefore, the greater its competitive advantage over rivals. Also, being known as a destination that utilizes "copy-cat strategies," rather than "innovative strategies," does little for a one's image. Progressive conservative destinations tend to take the reactive position of quickly following innovators—after it has been established that the new product or service is viable and profitable.

Passive

Passive destinations, generally those in Positions 4 and 5, simply do what they have been doing with little or no focus on changes in their competitive environment. There are two basic types of passive destinations: Position 1 or 2 destinations, and destinations in Positions 3 through 5. After a destination moves up to Position 1 or 2, it must generally take a respite of about one year to allow customers to get used to the new offering and for the destination to maximize its new image. There would be little point in making aggressive changes after achieving this position. Instead, efficiencies through standardization of strategies, high revenues, and cost minimization are the focus of strategic efforts. Proactiveness and even reactiveness are discouraged because this would be counterproductive to management's abilities and philosophies. Passive destinations may follow the lead of reactive organizations, but only after the success of the strategic change is unquestionably evident and revenues have shown a significant downward trend (Miller, 1994). Occasionally, there will be a market for passive destinations. When, for example, the elderly constitute a primary market, the destination can often successfully pursue passivity because this is what its market expects.

Adaptive

These destinations choose to be flexible to allow them to adapt to their relatively stable environment. Sometimes this level of aggression is chosen by Position 1 or 2 destinations when management wants to continue with its current highly or reasonably successful strategies but remain open to appropriate changes if the right opportunity presents itself. This works because the location has acquired the image of Position 1 or 2 and can rest on its current reputation until it is ready to pursue a more aggressive strategy or market demand for its current product mix or promotional efforts begin to weaken. This does not mean that the environment is ignored; management simply chooses to be opportunistic about its strategic moves. In some cases, rather than make major strategy decisions during annual planning meetings, adaptive managers will make minor strategy decisions throughout the year. Some destinations in Position 3 or 4 may select this strategy because they are satisfied that their current position is probably as high as their resources and management can take them.

The adaptive level of strategic aggression differs from the reactive level because the destination is not aggressively following the actions of proactive tourism bureaus. It is instead searching for the most suitable strategy for its specific circumstance. This new strategy could be proactive or reactive, but it could also have the purpose of simply keeping the destination in its present desired position. The adaptive level differs from the passive level in that the destination is actively monitoring its market in pursuit of potential strategies; it has simply not found an appropriate option.

Discordant

The discordant destination will usually be in Position 4 or 5. It has had problems with past strategic decisions and is unsure about how to deal with its current position, particularly deciding where its best opportunities lie. This strategy is not selected, but acquired through poor performance. The causes vary, but include disagreements between tourism bureau personnel, doing too many things at once, misconceptions about the environment, preconceived (personal) strategic agendas, analysis paralysis (fear of action), and ineffective implementation efforts. Discordant destinations are generally in need of a turnaround but unfortunately may not realize it until it is too late. These destinations are in need of a coordinated strategy that addresses the specific reasons for its current problems.

Past, Present, and Future Changes in Aggression and Position

A further application of the strategic aggression analysis is the study of how a destination's present position can influence future strategic aggression choices, and subsequently how these choices can influence the destination's future position. Destinations that have been complacent or attempted to minimize risk in their strategic choices and have subsequently not achieved their desired positions may want to consider more aggressive strategic options (see Figures 4.8 and 4.9).

In Figure 4.8 it can be seen that each destination has certain realistic options available to it based on its current position. These strategic aggression choices will result in some type of modification to its position. An additional application of this concept is to assist in forecasting competitors, strategic actions. An important domain assumption for this model is that it will be possible to change a destination's position based on its tenure at its current position. For example, a destination in one position generally cannot select a higher than normal level of aggression and expect to reach the position most often associated with that level of aggression. If a destination in Position 3 selects a Level 1 or proactive level of strategic aggression, it will not likely result in vaulting it to Position 1 (see Figure 4.9). The reason is that this Position 3 destination has normally been there for some time and therefore has acquired the image of this position. Therefore, it will be difficult to convince its target market that it has gone from being an average option to being one of the best options. Assuming that the proactive strategy was implemented effectively, the most likely result would be to raise the destination to Position 2. This model can also assist in forecasting competitors' strategic actions.

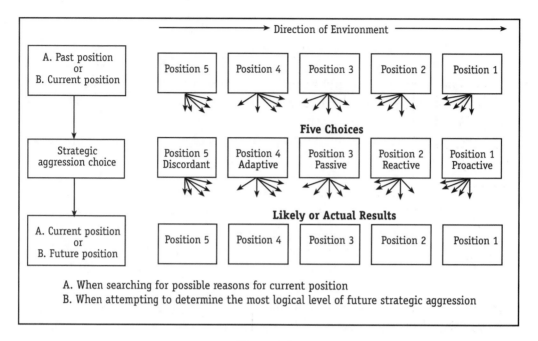

Figure 4.8:
Position-strategic aggression sequence for tourist destinations

STEP #5. SELECT A POSITIONING OR REPOSITIONING STRATEGY

Up to this point management has gathered information on: (a) its target customers' desired attributes, (b) the destination's and its competitors' performance and current positions, (c) the desired future position for the geographic area and forecasted positions of competitors, and (d) the appropriate level of strategic aggression. Now management must begin the process of deciding which attributes should be focused on to achieve this desired position. For planning purposes, the positioning or repositioning strategy is expressed in a positioning statement.

Since there will almost always be an effort to incrementally improve the destination's position, a decision must be made on the relevance of current market research and information. If research efforts have not provided possible options, then personnel must re-analyze existing data to determine if something was overlooked or if new research data is required.

Before positioning decisions are made, management must thoroughly understand its attributes and review environmental factors to learn about the

> **B**efore positioning decisions are made, management must thoroughly understand its attributes and review environmental factors to learn about the unique needs (attributes) of its targeted markets.

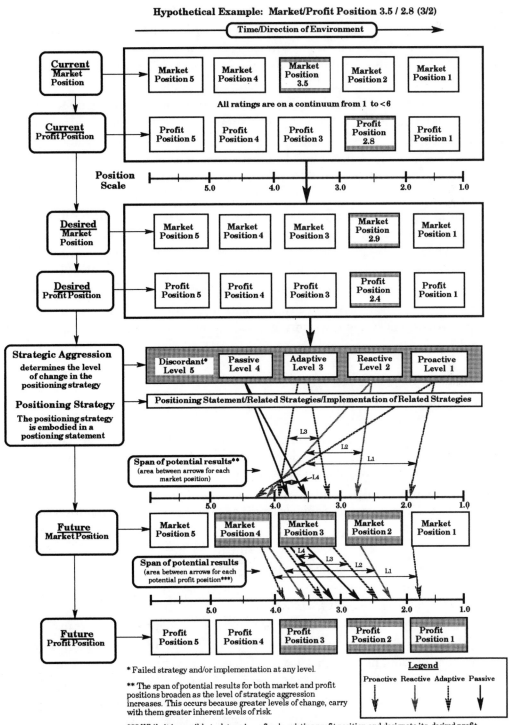

Figure 4.9:
Market/profit position—strategic aggression positioning strategy sequence

unique needs (attributes) of its targeted markets. The goal is to satisfy customers in a manner that lets the destination stand out from the multitude of competing destinations. When there is no cost-effective way to compete head-on with a larger competitor, a position focused on this competitor's weakest points could be considered. Another alternative would be to develop creative ways of serving customers that would likely not be adopted by these larger competitors (Stalk et al., 1992). Some of the key considerations for deciding on a position in the market are service quality (tangibles, reliability, responsiveness, assurance, and empathy), product quality, customization, quantity, variety, consistency, convenience, value (ideally package pricing), technology, delivery speed and efficiency, meaningful changes or additions, and image (Lee & Hing, 1995; Parasuraman, Zeithaml, & Berry, 1988; Reich, 1990).

A central issue in positioning is that if a geographic destination is positioned behind competitors, then special promotions or reduced prices will be the only means of maintaining sales. Unfortunately, this attempt at sales maintenance will come at the expense of lower profit margins, lower property valuations, and strategic instability. Promotions of various types will always be necessary for destinations; however, the greater the reliance on a strong market position, the easier it will be to attract guests without heavy discounting and high relative promotional expenditures.

Positioning and Implementation

Positioning is based primarily on the aggregate position of the tourist-oriented destinations in the trade area, transportation costs, travel trends (popular geographic regions and distance), public relation and promotional efforts, political stability, and the area's current reputation. However, the true measure of a position is not determined exclusively by strategy selection, but also by how well customers perceive the geographic destination to have delivered on their positioning decisions. For this reason, implementation of strategies is as important as the strategies themselves (Calantone & Manzanec, 1991). Promises made must be delivered upon.

A skilled hotel sales manager will make sure that a meeting goes well by monitoring each service the hotel provides. Similarly, the management of a tourism bureau must make sure that guests of their destination enjoy their stay and have their expectations met or exceeded. Obviously, the task of the hotel sales manager will generally be more controllable than that of a manager with a tourism bureau. The major difference is that the bureau's management cannot monitor every group that visits their destination, nor can they feel confident that every hotel or other tourist organization will provide quality-oriented service (Calantone & Manzanec, 1991). A tourism bureau will be spinning its wheels promoting a destination with subpar facilities. Generally, its efforts will be best spent enlisting the cooperation of as many tourism-related destinations as possible in professional associations. Setting standards and sponsoring training sessions can assist in improving the destination's performance and therefore its position. Additionally, the bureau should be responsible for coordinating the destination's promotions, making sure that they stand out from competing offers, and are cost effective.

Positioning Maps

Positioning maps (also perceptual maps or multidimensional scaling) show how the market perceives a certain set of destinations based on their performance on selected attributes/variables (Lewis, 1985). While there are many types of positioning maps, the two general categories are *decompositional positioning maps,* comparisons between different brands, and *compositional positioning maps,* comparisons of the attributes of a single destination (Steenkamp, Trijp, & Ten Berge, 1994). Their purpose is to show how the market perceives a certain set of brands (destinations) or products. Each destination competes based on how the market views its products as being close substitutes for other products. The positioning map graphs the spacial relationship between the products or brands based on specified attributes. The closer the distance between two products or destinations, the closer the market's perceived relationship. In addition to helping determine the destination's most suitable position, they can also be used to track actual market changes and potential market changes, such as when a new product or strategy is being proposed (Dillon, Madden, & Firtle, 1987). Generally, data for the positioning maps will come from survey information. When survey data are not available, then management's best judgment is a common alternative.

Most positioning maps are based on a four-quadrant matrix that is made up of two axes and multiple coordinates or scores. The axes specify the dimensions that the destinations or products will be judged on. The coordinates represent the position of each brand (product) on the axes. When descriptive statistics are used, the coordinates (plot points) are the mean responses for each attribute (variable). Frequently graphed attributes include price and product quality; room rate and room quality, features, or appearance; price and service quality; price/room rate and location; convention/meeting facilities and room rate; convention/meeting facilities and location; convenience and quality; convenience and price; or service quality and food quality (Reich, 1997a). If more variables are desired, then several positioning maps can be created, possibly one with room rate and room quality, and others with room rate and amenities, or location and amount of meeting space. When necessary, it is acceptable to use a form of factor analysis to combine related variables into one category. A restaurant could combine portion size, flavor, taste, and plate appearance into one variable, food quality. A hotel could similarly combine courtesy of front desk staff with that of their restaurants, banquets, housekeeping, concierge, and bellpersons into the variable service. These attributes can be combined by adding their means, then dividing by the number of variables that were factored together. For an in-depth discussion of positioning maps, see Cravens (1994) and Haahti (1986).

Awareness and Image

Two positioning maps that are helpful in highlighting a destination's marketing image are brand awareness/brand loyalty and image/attribute importance (Barich & Kotler, 1991). In Figure 4.10, brand awareness and brand image are plotted for four different hotels. Hotel A's customers view it favorably, but it has not maximized its awareness. Hotel B is currently in the ideal position and should consider growth strategies that allow it to capitalize on its position. Few of Hotel C's target customers are aware that it exists and those that are do not consider it as a first option. Before this hotel would attempt to solve its awareness problem, it must first find out what it is doing wrong internally. The advantage of hotels over restaurants in this quadrant is that while potential hotel guests are dispersed throughout large geographic areas, a restaurant's market is in a narrowly defined trade area. The hotel in this position could correct some of their problems, then focus on attracting new guests. A restaurant, because of the increased likelihood of exposure to its target customer base, would generally not be in this quadrant. If it was located here, like the hotel, it must first correct problems before attempting to attract new customers. Hotel D is in the worst position by far. Its customers are not happy with its performance and the majority of its target market is aware of this fact. Here, the destination will not only need to improve its internal standards, but it will need to focus heavily on promotions targeted at reversing its negative image. A restaurant in this quadrant may have alienated too large of percentage of its potential market to allow it to make a few changes then attempt to attract the same individuals again.

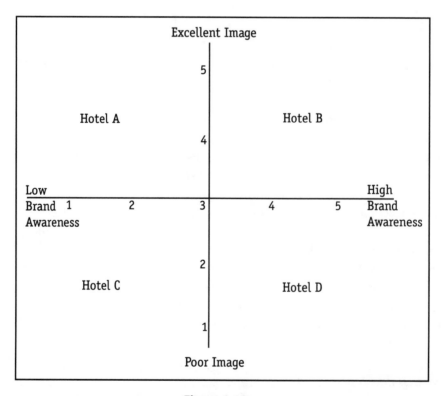

Figure 4.10:
Awareness/image positioning map for hotels A, B, C, & D

Adapted from: Barich, H., & Kotler, P. (1991). A framework for marketing image management. *Sloan Management Review, 32*(2), 94-104.

Figure 4.11, an image/attribute importance position map, shows how company A compares on several key attributes with its closest rival, company B. Company A's different positions would first be analyzed based on why they are where they are, then second based on their comparison to company B. Positioning strategies would subsequently be developed that improve the destination's current position relative to competitors. It is always best to work with prioritized attributes, so that management can focus on those most critical to success. It should also be remembered that since positioning primarily concerns the destination's overall image, all relevant attributes must be considered.

Focused Attribute Positioning Maps

In the positioning map in Figure 4.12, the owner of Gabriel's Burgers and Malts is trying to decide where the restaurant should be positioned based on the attributes of quality and value. Since the customer market consists primarily of business professionals, Gabriel feels that these would be the main determinants of customer choice. His initial thought when he opened was to offer a good-quality burger at a low price. Because of this initial desired position, he would have to carefully consider Competitor B's high quality-high value position. If a similar of-

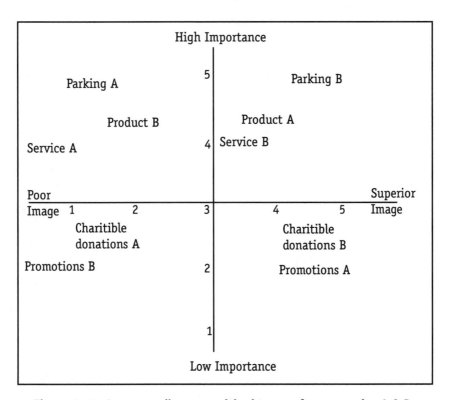

Figure 4.11: Awareness/image positioning map for companies A & B

Adapted from: Barich, H., & Kotler, P. (1991). A framework for marketing image management. *Sloan Management Review, 32*(2), 94-104.

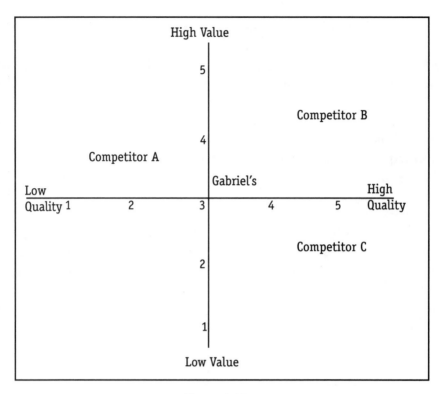

Figure 4.12:
Awareness/image positioning map for Gabriel's Restaurant and competitors A, B, & C

Adapted from: Barich, H., & Kotler, P. (1991). A framework for marketing image management. *Sloan Management Review, 32*(2), 94-104.

fering to Competitor B's were made, then, because of a lack of differentiation, it may be difficult to draw customers away from B. Gabriel must determine if it is worth his effort or if it would be possible to develop a product and value mix that is superior to B, or if it would be better to find another position to concentrate on (Kiefer & Kelly, 1995). If Competitor C was successful and customers appeared not to mind paying a higher price for a good burger, perhaps Gabriel's current position between Competitors B and C would be a prudent choice. Competitor A would likely be only of minimal importance unless for some reason its sales, relative to the competition, were above average. If this were the case, then new information, that of quality not being a major determinant of choice for some target customers, would be considered in the positioning decision.

In Figure 4.13, the sales managers in the sales and marketing department of the Mountain View Hotel ranked three competitors along the determinant attributes of size of meeting space and value. For the Mountain View Hotel to decide on a new position in this particular market, it might consider the following analysis. Competitor C is viewed as the worst value. For group business, this hotel would only be a major competitor for large conventions and probably only during the off-season. Positioning against Competitor B would involve emphasizing Mountain

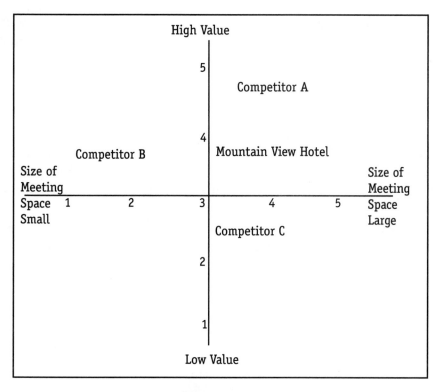

Figure 4.13:
Awareness/image positioning map for group business for
the Mountain View Hotel and competitors A, B & C

Adapted from: Barich, H., & Kotler, P. (1991). A framework for marketing image management. *Sloan Management Review, 32*(2), 94-104.

View's advantage in meeting space at a relatively comparable value. Competitor A has similar meeting space characteristics, but its value is substantially higher. The question here would be, "Why?" Are the meeting rooms larger, better furnished or does the hotel have a better overall image? To position itself against Competitor A, the Mountain View Hotel will have to either lower its rates, or if it wants to keep its current rate structure intact, emphasize features that could improve its value perception. These could include an emphasis on customization capabilities, quality of food or service, location, view, ground transportation, physical facilities, and so on.

Plotting a Positioning Map

Any scale can be adapted to a positioning map; the simplest is to stay with the common 5- or 7-point preference scale (the axes are at 3 and 4 respectively). Another method is to consider one's business as the axis position, then rate competitor's attributes as being stronger (a rating of +1 = marginally stronger to +5 = much stronger) or weaker (a rating of -1 = marginally weaker to -5 = much weaker). A variation is to rank one's business on the same -5 to +5 scale as that of competitors with the axis at 0 and representing a neutral or average response. If these alternative methods of plotting a positioning map are utilized, the measurement procedure for the survey instrument should be modified to assure compatibility. Multidimensional scaling with the use of statistical software package can also be used to create positioning maps.

Position Decision Matrix

This analysis allows for comparisons between two or more geographic destinations on multiple attributes. Its main purpose is to provide a format for marketers to determine how critical factors should be incorporated into the organization's positioning statement. Secondarily, it guides the development of functional strategies that lead to the destination's new position. For example, in Figure 4.14, the image of the two destinations is similar. Image improvement could be focused on, but there are problems with hotel quality that should be addressed before the destination's image is promoted. In this matrix, hotel quality is by far the most serious issue. Likewise, value should be addressed, since it is lower than the competitor's ranking. The focus of managers of these hotel properties will be the

Recommended attribute	Destination's standing (1-5)	Competitor's standing (1-5)	Importance of improving standing (H-M-L)*	Ability to improve (H-M-L)	Competitor's ability to improve (H-M-L)	Action
Image of geographic destination	4.3	4.1	M	M	L	Hold
Overall average quality of hotels	3.4	3.2	H	H	M	Improve quality
Overall average value of hotels	4.3	4.5	H	H	M	Focus
Variety of activities	4.7	4.3	L	L	M	Hold
Political stability	4.4	3.5	M	L	L	Monitor
Transportation cost to destination	4.0	4.0	M	M	M	Focus
*H = High, M = Medium, L = Low						

Figure 4.14:
Position decision matrix

Adapted from: Kotler, P. (1991). *Marketing management: Analysis, planning, implementation, & control.* Englewood Cliffs, NJ: Prentice-Hall, p. 305.

effective operation and positioning of their individual organizations. However, they must be convinced that participation in area tourism efforts is critical to both the success of their organization and that of the geographic destination (Jamal & Getz, 1995; Selin & Chavez, 1995). Air transportation costs to the destination are in the same range as the competing destination and are viewed as being less satisfactory than most other categories. Perhaps, promotional packages that lower prices and therefore price resistance may help.

Similarly, in this matrix, the company scored higher than its competitor in atmosphere, cleanliness, and points of differentiation categories. While each of these categories are important to customers, they do not have equal appeal for purposes of positioning. For most restaurants the average customer will prefer good food and service over atmosphere. So while atmosphere is important, it may not be a critical issue in the positioning decision. Cleanliness, again, is an important issue for customers, but this is expected as a minimum standard of operating a restaurant. If this was a major concern to the target customer, then it could tactfully be included in advertising by showing a bright, spotless restaurant. Some destinations owe a portion of their success to having facilities that are much cleaner than their competitors. A riskier approach in this situation would be some type of comparison between the company's clean restaurant and a hypothetical restaurant that happens to be quite dirty. The fact that the restaurant serves fresh bread, large portions, and has an exhibition kitchen would likely help the restaurant's image, and should therefore be included in the positioning decision.

POSITIONING STATEMENTS

Geographic destinations will need one general positioning statement and possibly several additional positioning statements if they cater to two or more market segments. Target segments could include business transient (individual business traveler), leisure (tourist), and group, as well as different income segments. A sample overall positioning statement for a destination follows along with statements for various targeted segments. The format for a hotel's positioning statement would be the same. The primary difference would be the variables utilized.

Sample Destination Positioning Statements

Overall

We are a lush tropical island, offering guests a wide variety of vacation, business, and conference options. Just a short flight from Miami, Florida, guests are transported back in time to a getaway that lives up to its name. Mountainous jungle terrain, beautiful birds, friendly little animals, and white sandy beaches provide the change of scenery that will calm even the most stressed executive. Whether you're on a budget or have just closed a big deal, our island has the facilities to please everyone.

Travel Intermediaries

Travel agents, tour operators, meeting planners, and reservation services can be assured of first-class service. In fact, it is our government and tourist bureau policy to be the obvious choice for travel intermediaries desiring dependability, honesty, and quality in all transactions. All commissions from the island are paid within 30 days, if not sooner. With one of the most proactive democratic governments in the Atlantic, a comprehensive and dependable transportation system, and a professional tourism support staff, we are ready to assist in your every need. We want our guests to relax and enjoy our lush tropical island, not worry about dealing with problems.

Business Groups

Though our island is a lush tropical hideaway, we have three, 350-plus-room hotels with an extraordinary level of business-class service, at a highly competitive rate. With names like the Hilton, Marriott, and the five-star Island Palace, you can be assured of the best possible setting as key decisions are made. When the business is done, there are activities for all ages from sports and world-class shopping, to some of the region's best entertainment venues and museums.

Leisure

Our lush tropical island offers a wide variety of sporting activities, including jogging, horseback riding, hiking, an indoor/outdoor swimming pool, scuba and snorkeling, tennis, and golf. For shoppers we have one of the largest outdoor markets in the territory. You can find deals on leather goods, jewelry, cotton clothing, pottery, and many other fine quality products. Our museums, restaurants, and nightlife will assure you of a fun getaway at an affordable price.

Restaurant Positioning Statements

Positioning decisions will be somewhat simpler for restaurants than for hotels. Restaurants will generally focus on between one (fine dining) and perhaps two or three target groups (casual dining and fast-food) with a relatively homogeneous product—its menu, services, pricing, and atmosphere. They will, of course, offer products that will be desired by a small number of members of other target groups, but there are generally very few changes that must be made to accommodate these secondary target groups. Perhaps a special menu for children, lower prices for senior citizens, or one or two entrees for smaller targeted groups. The positioning statement is written as a guide for the setting of marketing strategies. It must answer the question of how the business wants to be viewed by customers relative to competitors. The following is a sample positioning statement for a restaurant:

Typical Restaurant Positioning Statement
We serve a variety of fresh seafood,
including shrimp, crab, lobster, and a minimum of
10 varieties of fish. Preparation methods include

broiled, baked, grilled, blackened, steamed, and fried.
Salad, baked potato, a choice from three vegetables,
and fresh bread will be offered with each meal.
Cooks must be trained in the intricacies of seafood preparation. We have a
full-service bar with a premium well.
Service is casual, but very professional. Prices are
moderate and will be slightly above our competition to
allow for higher quality products. As much as possible,
fish will be purchased from day boats. Promotion will
be held to a minimum, focusing on employee contests
and public relations.
We want to be thought of as *seafood experts.*

Hotel Positioning Statements

Hotels will need one general positioning statement and possibly several individual positioning statements if the hotel caters to two or more market segments.
An average hotel could have four or more target segments such as business transient
(individual business traveler), leisure (tourist), group, and catering. A sample overall positioning statement follows along with statements for various targeted segments:

We are a quality hotel that offers competitively
priced rooms and food, a broad array of meeting
and banquet services, a casual restaurant that
serves three meals, and a variety of recreational
facilities. Our lobby will emphasize relaxation
with comfortable couches arranged for informal
meetings, beverage service, and an abundance of
live plants. All employees will be trained to deliver
"friendly service" that cannot be equaled in our market.

• Individual Business Travelers: A full-service hotel that is conveniently located in the Williamsburg area, with immediate access to interstate highway 45,
near suburban and downtown business districts, and provides travelers an extraordinary level of business-class services at a highly competitive rate.

• Tourists: A full-service hotel with a variety of activities, including jogging
trails, hiking, an indoor/outdoor swimming pool, tennis, and shopping in one of
the largest malls in the Southwest. Major league sports, first-class museums, a lively
theater district, an exceptional variety of live music, and exceptional restaurants
help assure a fun getaway at an affordable price.

• Groups: We are a full-service hotel offering everything necessary for a successful group function, from modern facilities, exceptional personalized service,
on-property recreation facilities, and a location accessible to local airports, shopping, and highways. The hotel is located in a dynamic city with activities for all ages
from sports activities and world-class shopping, to some of the country's best edu-

cational entertainment venues and museums. The individual guest's satisfaction with our hotel is a commitment of all employees.

• Catering and Banquets: We provide catered events that exceed guests' expectations in quality of service, food and beverage, and atmosphere, at a price that represents a great value. An extensive catering menu will be available to serve the needs of guests in the middle to upper-middle income range. The hotel will be capable of a variety of functions from the traditional, to special events and theme parties.

Positioning Slogans

Often a slogan, a brief and memorable summary of the destination's desired position, can be written. Its purpose is to help communicate the business's positioning strategy and help to influence and support its overall image. The first step would be to decide what is it that customers want most that the business can supply better than competitors, or at least be convinced of this. The previous restaurant positioning statement offers an obvious possibility, "Seafood experts." A hotel could adopt a portion of its positioning statement for its positioning slogan, "The Bryan House, a first-class value in a business-class hotel." The slogan would then be used on signage, stationery, in advertising and other promotions.

Strategies Supportive of the Position

Once the positioning decision has been made, management will then be faced with the task of deciding how it will utilize various functional strategies and tactics (tactics include action plans and policies) to support the position. Previously gathered information from the market position analysis, positioning maps, and the positioning decision matrix should be re-assessed for relevance.

> *Often a slogan, a brief and memorable summary of the destination's desired position, can be written. Its purpose is to help communicate the business's positioning strategy and help to influence and support its overall image.*

Since many of the attributes that management has decided to focus on are expressed in the positioning statement, the essential task is to prepare strategies and tactics that guide their implementation. To accomplish this task, management must measure its performance on each specific attribute, then determine what changes are necessary to reach the performance level as expressed in the positioning statement. Previously gathered information from the market position analysis, positioning maps, and the positioning decision matrix should be re-assessed as these decisions are made.

Positioning and the Mission

The destination's positioning decisions, like the mission statement, help establish the foundation for objectives and strategy decisions developed in the marketing or strategic plan. But there are differences. The mission statement could be viewed as the destination's attempt to position itself for the long-term future, perhaps the next five or more years, while the destination's positioning decisions are targeted more at meeting the shorter-term demands of its markets (at least for the next year and possibly up to about two years). Consequently, the portion of the mission statement that covers product and market characteristics is somewhat general to allow for flexibility in strategic direction and quick responses to new opportunities. The positioning of the destination will state more explicitly where the destination would like to be in the short-term future, specifying in greater detail what products, services, and other strategies will be utilized for each target group. For example, a mission statement for a restaurant could include a description of the product: "A casual seafood restaurant specializing in high-quality fresh seafood." The positioning statement would usually, but not necessarily, be more explicit, including those features that the target market considers important. This could include such details as the quality of the seafood, how it will be procured, stored, inventoried, and prepared (see the previous restaurant positioning statement).

CONCLUSION

When developing strategic or marketing plans for tourism destinations, it is imperative that positioning be given adequate attention. It should be viewed as the junction point or funnel between the destination's research (situational analysis) and its functional-level strategies. From the mission statement the destination knows where it wants to be in the long term, positioning establishes the guidelines for the short-term steps necessary to get there. Since the destination's position comprises much of the basis for customers to decide between one business and another, an increased focus on the positioning process is well worth the effort. The process proposed in this book is relatively simple, requiring five basic steps. The primary additions to the traditional positioning process are the concepts of linear positioning and strategic aggression.

The implication of these concepts are that they: (a) establish a hierarchical relationship of primary competitors, (b) show how this relationship has changed in the past and how it might change in the future, and (c) help management determine the overall degree of change necessary to achieve the destination's ideal position. These steps provide management a graphic and logical process for future positioning and strategy efforts.Positioning techniques presented here can be applied to any hospitality, related product.

References

Aaker, D. A. (1988). *Strategic market management* (2nd ed.). New York: John Wiley & Sons.

Abelson, R. P. (1964). Modes of resolution of belief dilemmas. In M. Fishbein (Ed.), *Readings in attitude theory and management* (pp. 349-356). New York: John Wiley & Sons.

Abelson R. P., & Rosenberg, M. J. (1964). Symbolic psycho-logic: A model of attitudinal cognition. *Behavioral Science, 3,* 1-8.

Abernathy, W. J., & Utterback, J. M. (1978, June-July). Patterns of industrial innovation. *Technology Review, 10,* 41-47.

Adler, L. (1968). A new orientation for plotting marketing strategy. In R. L. Day (Ed.), *Concepts for modern marketing* (pp. 304-322). Scranton, PA: International Textbook.

Ajzen, I., & Fishbein, M. (1980). *Understanding attitudes and predicting social behavior.* Englewood Cliffs, NJ: Prentice-Hall.

Alba, J. W., & Chattopadhyay, A. (1986). Salience effects in brand recall. *Journal of Marketing Research, 23,* 363-369.

Alderson, W. (1957). *Marketing behavior and executive action: A functionalist approach to marketing theory.* Homewood, IL: Irwin.

Alderson, W. (1965). *Dynamic marketing behavior: A functionalist theory of marketing.* Homewood, IL: Irwin.

Allport, G. W. (1935). *A handbook of social psychology.* Clark University Press.

Anderson, J. R. (1983). *The architecture of cognition.* Cambridge, MA: Harvard University Press.

Ankomah, P. K., Crompton, J. L., & Baker, D. (1996). Influence of cognitive distance in vacation choice. *Annals of Tourism Research, 23,* 138-150.

Assael, H. (1985). *Marketing management: Strategy and action.* Boston: Kent Publishing.

Barich, H., & Kotler, P. (1991). A framework for marketing image management. *Sloan Management Review, 32*(2), 94-104.

Barsky, J. D. (1992). Customer satisfaction in the hotel industry: Meaning and measurement. *Hospitality Research Journal, 16*(1), 51-73.

Bateson, J. E. G. (1989). Managing services marketing. Chicago: Dryden Press.

Blumer, H. (1955). Attitudes and the social act. *Social Problems, 3,* 59-64.

Bonn, M. A., & Brand, R. R. (1995). Identifying market potential: The application of brand development indexing to pleasure travel. *Journal of Travel Research, 34*(2), 31-35.

Bowles, M. L. (1991). The organization shadow. *Organization Studies, 12,* 387-404.

Boyd, H. W., Jr., & Walker, O. C., Jr. (1990). *Marketing management: A strategic approach.* Homewood, IL: Irwin.

Bramwell, B., & Rawding, L. (1996). Tourism marketing images of industrial cities. *Annals of Tourism Research, 23,* 201-221.

Brown, J. S. (1991). Research that reinvents the corporation. *Harvard Business Review, 69*(1), 102-111.

Calantone, R. J., & Mazanec, J. A. (1991). Marketing management and tourism. *Annals of Tourism Research, 18,* 101-119.

Callan, R. J. (1994). Development of a framework for the determination of attributes used for hotel selection—indications from focus group and in-depth interviews. *Hospitality Research Journal, 18*(2), 53-74.

Callan, R. J. (1995). Hotel classification and grading schemes, a paradigm of utilization and user characteristics. *International Journal of Hospitality Management, 14*(3/4), 271-284.

Carpenter, G. S., Glazer, R., & Nakamoto, K. (1994). Meaningful brands from meaningless differentiation: The dependence on irrelevant attributes. *Journal of Marketing Research, 31*(3), 339-350.

Churchill, G. A. Jr. (1979). A paradigm for developing better measures of marketing constructs. *Journal of Marketing Research, 16,* 64-73.

Cohen, J. B., Fishbein, M., & Ahtola, O. T. (1972). The nature and uses of expectancy-value models in consumer attitude research. *Journal of Marketing Research, 9,* 456-460.

Cooper, L. G., & Inoue, A. (1996). Building market structures from consumer preferences. *Journal of Marketing Research, 33,* 293-306.

Covin, J. G. (1991). Entrepreneurial versus conservative firms: A comparison of strategies and performance. *Journal of Management Studies, 28*(5), 439-462.

Cravens, D. W. (1991). *Strategic marketing.* Homewood, IL: Irwin.

Cronin, J. J. Jr., & Taylor, S. A. (1992). Measuring service quality: A reexamination and extension. *Journal of Marketing, 56*(3), 55-68.

Cundiff, E. W., & Still, R. R. (1964). *Basic marketing: Concepts, environment, and decisions.* Englewood Cliffs, NJ: Prentice-Hall.

Curry, D. J. (1985). Measuring price and quality competition. *Journal of Marketing, 2*(49), 106-117.

Davis, D., & Cosenza, R. M. (1988). *Business research for decision making.* Boston: PWS-Kent Publishing.

Day, G. S., & Wensley, R. (1988). Assessing advantage: A framework for diagnosing competitive superiority. *Journal of Marketing, 52*(2), 1-20.

Deighton, J., Henderson, C. M., & Neslin, S. A. (1994). The effects of advertising on brand switching and repeat purchasing. *Journal of Marketing Research, 31*(1), 28-43.

Dev, C. S., Morgan, M. S. & Shoemaker, S. (1995). A positioning analysis of hotel brands: Based on travel-manager perceptions. *Cornell Hotel and Restaurant Administration Quarterly, 36*(6), 48-55.

Dichter, E. (1964). *Handbook of consumer motivations.* New York: McGraw-Hill.

Dickson, J. P. & MacLachlan, D. L. (1990). Social distance and shopping behavior. *Journal of the Academy of Marketing Science, 18*(2), 153-161.

Dillon, W. R., Madden, T. J., & Firtle, N. H. (1987). *Marketing research in a marketing environment* (2nd ed.). Homewood, IL: Irwin.

DiMingo, E. (1988). The fine art of positioning. *The Journal of Business Strategy, 9*(2), 34-38.

Dodson, J. (1991). Strategic repositioning through the customer connection. *The Journal of Business Strategy, 12* (3), 34-38.

Doob, L. W. (1947). The behavior of attitudes. *Psychological Review, 54,* 135-156.

Drucker, P. F. (1985). The discipline of innovation. *Harvard Business Review, 85*(3), 67-72.

Dunn, S. W., & Barban, A. M. (1978). *Advertising: Its role in modern marketing* (4th ed.). Hinsdale, IL: Dryden.

Echtner, C. M., & Ritchie, J. R. B. (1993). The measurement of destination image: An empirical assessment. *Journal of Travel Research, 31*(4), 3-13.

Edwards, A. L. (1957). *The social desirability variable in personality assessment and research.* New York: Dryden.

Embacher, J., & Buttle, F. (1989). A repertory grid analysis of Austria's image as a summer vacation destination. *Journal of Travel Research, 27*(3), 3-7.

Feltenstein, T. (1986). New-product development in food service: A structured approach. *The Cornell Hotel and Restaurant Administration Quarterly, 27*(3), 63-71.

Festinger, L. (1957). *A theory of cognitive dissonance.* Stanford, CA: Stanford University Press.

Filiatrault, P., & Ritchie, J. R. B. (1988). The impact of situational factors on the evaluation of hospitality services. *Journal of Travel Research, 24*(3), 29-37.

Fishbein, M. A. (1967). Attitude and the prediction of behavior. In M. Fishbein (Ed.), *Readings in attitude theory and measurement* (pp. 477-492). New York: John Wiley.

Fridgen, J. D. (1987). Use of cognitive maps to determine perceived tourism regions. *Leisure Sciences, 9,* 101-117.

Galbraith, C., & Schendel, D. (1983). An empirical analysis of strategy types. *Strategic Management Journal, 4,* 153-173.

Gartner, W. C. (1989, Fall)). Tourism image: Attribute measurement of state tourism products using multidimensional scaling techniques. *Journal of Travel Research,* 16-20.

Gartner, W. C. (1993). Image formation process. In M. Uysal & D. F. Fesenmaier (Eds.), *Communication and channel systems in tourism marketing.* Binghamton, NY: Haworth.

Gartner, W. C., & Hunt, J. D. (1987, Fall)). An analysis of state image change over a twelve-year period (1971-1983). *Journal of Travel Research*, 15-19.

Getty, J. M., & Thompson, K. N. (1994). A procedure for scaling perceptions of lodging quality. *Hospitality Research Journal, 18*(2), 75-96.

Ginter, P. M., & White, D. D. (1982). A social learning approach to strategic management: Toward a theoretical foundation. *Academy of Management Review, 7*(2), 253-261.

Green, D. H., Barclay, D. W., & Ryans, A. B. (1995). Entry strategy and long-term performance: conceptualization and empirical examination. *Journal of Marketing, 59*(4), 1-16.

Gunn, C. (1972). *Vacationscape: Designing tourist regions.* Austin, TX: University of Texas, Bureau of Business Research.

Guralnik, D. B. (1986). *Webster's new world dictionary of the American language.* New York: Prentice-Hall.

Guttman, L. (1950). The problem of attitude and opinion measurement: The basis of scalogram analysis. In S. A. Stoufer, et al., *Measurement and prediction: Studies in social psychology in World War II* (vol. 4). 46-90. Princeton, NJ: Princeton University Press.

Haahti, A. J. (1986). Finland's competitive position as a destination. *Annals of Tourism Research, 13*(1), 11-35.

Hair, J. F., Jr., Anderson, R. E., Tatham, & Black, W. C. (1995). *Multivariate data analysis* (4th. ed.). Englewood Cliffs, NJ: Prentice-Hall.

Haywood, K. M. (1986). Scouting the competition for survival and success. *The Cornell Hotel and Restaurant Administration Quarterly, 27*(3), 81-87.

Heider, F. (1946). Attitudes and cognitive organization. *Journal of Psychology, 21*, 107-112.

Herbig, P., & Milewicz, J. (1993). The relationship of reputation and credibility to brand success. *Journal of Consumer Marketing, 10*(3), 18-24.

Heskett, J. L. (1984). *Managing in the service economy.* Boston: Harvard Business School Press.

Hill, T., & Shaw, R. N. (1995). Co-marketing tourism internationally: Bases for strategic alliances. *Journal of Travel Research, 34*(1), 25-32.

Howard, J. A. (1983). Market theory of the firm. *Journal of Marketing, 47*(4), 90-100.

Hunt, S. D., & Morgan, R. M. (1995). The comparative advantage theory of competition. *Journal of Marketing, 59*(2), 1-15.

Hurley, J. A. (1990). Highway hotel: Anatomy of a turnaround. *The Cornell Hotel and Restaurant Administration Quarterly, 31*(2), 36-44.

Ireland, R. D., Hitt, M. A., Bettis, R. A., & De Porras, D. A. (1987). Strategy formulation processes: Differences in perceptions of strengths and weaknesses indicators and environmental uncertainty by managerial level. *Strategic Management Journal, 8*, 469-485.

Jamal, T. B., & Getz, D. (1995). Collaboration theory and community tourism planning. *Annals of Tourism Research, 22*, 186-204.

Jeffrey, D., & Hubbard, N. J. (1994). A model of hotel occupancy performance for monitoring and marketing in the hotel industry. *International Journal of Hospitality Management, 13*(1), 57-71.

Jeffrey, D., & Xie, Y. (1995). The UK market for tourism in China. *Annals of Tourism Research, 22,* 857-876.

Kara, A., Kaynak, E., & Kucukemiroglu, O. (1995). Marketing strategies for fast-food restaurants: A customer view. *International Journal of Contemporary Hospitality Management, 7*(4), 16-22.

Keller, K. L. (1993). Conceptualizing, measuring, and managing customer-based brand equity. *Journal of Marketing, 57*(1), 1-22.

Kerlinger, F. N. (1973). *Foundations of behavioral research.* New York: Holt, Rinehart, and Winston.

Kerlinger, F. N. (1980). *Foundations of behavioral research* (2nd ed.). New York: Holt, Rinehart, and Winston.

Kiefer, N. M., & Kelly T. J. (1995). Price recollection and perceived value in restaurants. *Cornell Hotel and Restaurant Administration Quarterly, 36*(1), 47-56.

Kopalle, P. K., & Lehmann, D. R. (1995). The effects of advertised and observed quality on expectations about new product quality. *Journal of Marketing Research, 32,* 280-290.

Kotler, P. (1991). *Marketing management: Analysis, planning, implementation, & control* (7th ed,). Upper Saddle River, NJ: Prentice-Hall.

Kotler, P., Bowen, J., & Makens, J. (1996). *Marketing for hospitality and tourism.* Upper Saddle River, NJ: Prentice-Hall.

Kotler, P., & Armstrong, G. (1990). *Marketing, an introduction* (2nd ed.). Upper Saddle River, NJ: Prentice-Hall.

Krech, D., & Crutchfield, R. S. (1948). *Theory and problems of social psychology.* New York: McGraw-Hill.

Lamb, C. W., Hair, J. F. Jr., & McDaniel, C. (1994). *Principles of marketing* (2nd ed.). Cincinnati, OH: South-Western.

Lapidus, R. S., & Schibrowsky, J. A. (1994). Aggregate complaint analysis: A procedure for developing customer service satisfaction. *Journal of Services Marketing, 8*(4), 50-60.

Lee, L. L., & Hing, N. (1995). Measuring quality in restaurant operations: An application of the SERVQUAL instrument. *International Journal of Hospitality Management, 14*(3/4), 293-310.

Levitt, T. (1980). Marketing success through differentiation of anything. *Harvard Business Review, 58*(1), 83-91.

Lewis, R. C. (1981). The positioning statement for hotels. *The Cornell Hotel and Restaurant Administration Quarterly, 22,* 51-61.

Lewis, R. C. (1982). Positioning analysis for hospitality firms. *International Journal of Hospitality Management, 1*(2), 115-118.

Lewis, R. C. (1985). The market position: Mapping guest's perceptions of hotel operations. *The Cornell Hotel and Restaurant Administration Quarterly, 26*(2), 84-91.

Lewis, R. C. (1990). Advertising your hotel's position. *The Cornell Hotel and Restaurant Administration Quarterly, 31*(2), 84-91.

Lewis, R. C., Chambers, R. E., & Chacko, H. E. (1995). *Marketing leadership in hospitality: Foundations and practices.* New York: Van Nostrand Reinhold.

Lovelock, C. H. (1991). *Services marketing.* New York: Prentice-Hall.

Luck, D. J., & Rubin, R. S. (1987). *Marketing research* (7th ed.). Englewood Cliffs, NJ: Prentice-Hall.

Lutz, R. J. (1977). An experimental investigation of causal relations among cognitions, affect, and behavioral intention. *Journal of Consumer Research, 3,* 197-208.

McCarthy, E. J., & Perreault, W. D. Jr. (1993). *Basic marketing: A global-managerial approach* (11th ed.). Homewood, IL: Irwin.

McDowell, B. (1995). America's favorite chains. *Restaurants & Institutions, 105*(3), 52-72.

McGrath, J. E., Martin, J., & Kulka, R. A. (1982). *Judgment calls in research.* Beverly Hills, CA: Sage Publications.

McGuire, W. J. (1964). Modes of resolution of belief dilemmas. In M. Fishbein, *Readings in attitude theory and management* (pp. 357-365). New York: John Wiley.

McKee, D. O., Varadarajan, P. R., & Pride, W. M., (1989). Strategic adaptability and firm performance: A market-contingent perspective. *Journal of Marketing, 53*(3), 21-35.

Makridakis, S. (1991). What can we learn from corporate failure?. *Long Range Planning, 24* (4), 115-126.

Madrigal, R., & Kahle, L. R. (1994). Predicting vacation activity preference on the basis of value-system segmentation. *Journal of Travel Research, 32*(3), 22-28.

Mansfeld, Y. (1992). From motivation to actual travel. *Annals of Tourism Research, 19,* 399-419.

Martin, W. B. (1986a). Defining what quality service is for you. *The Cornell Hotel and Restaurant Administration Quarterly, 26*(4), 32-38.

Martin, W. B. (1986b). Measuring and improving your service quality. *The Cornell Hotel and Restaurant Administration Quarterly, 27*(1), 80-87.

Mayersohn, H. (1994). That dog won't hunt: Why what you've always done won't work anymore. *The Cornell Hotel and Restaurant Administration Quarterly, 35*(5), 82-87.

Mazanec, J. A. (1995, December). Positioning analysis with self-organizing maps. *Cornell Hotel and Restaurant Administration Quarterly,* 80-95.

Mazis, M. B., Ahtola, O. T., & Klippel, R. E. (1975). A comparison of four multiattribute models in the prediction of consumer attitudes. *Journal of Consumer Research, 2*(1), 38-52.

Miller, D. (1994). What happens after success: The perils of excellence. *Journal of Management Studies, 31*(3), 326-358.

Morrison, A. M. (1989). *Hospitality and travel marketing.* Albany, New York: Delmar Publishers.

Moutinho, L. (1987). Consumer behavior in tourism. *European Journal of Marketing, 21*(10), 1-44.

Muller, T. E. (1991); Using personal values to define segments in an international tourism market. *International Marketing Review, 1,* 57-70.

Nakanishi, M., & Bettman, J. R. (1974). Attitude models revisited: An individual level analysis. *Journal of Consumer Research 1*(3), 16-21.

Oliver, R. L. (1993). Cognitive, affective, and attribute bases of the satisfaction response. *Journal of Consumer Research, 20,* 418-430.

Oliver, R. L., & DeSarbo, W. S. (1988, March). Response determinants in satisfaction judgments. *Journal of Consumer Research, 12,* 495-507.

Oliver, R. L., & Swan, J. E. (1989, December). Equity and disconfirmation perceptions as influences on merchant and product satisfaction. *Journal of Consumer Research, 16,* 372-383.

Olsen, M. D., Tse, E. C., & West J. J. (1992). *Strategic Management in the Hospitality Industry.* New York: Van Nostrand Reinhold

Olson, E. M., Walker, O. C. Jr., & Ruekert, R. W. (1995). Organizing for effective new product development: the moderating role of product innovativeness. *Journal of Marketing, 59*(1), 48-62.

Palmer, A., & Bejou, D. (1995). Tourism destination marketing alliances. *Annals of Tourism Research, 22,* 616-629.

Parasuraman, A., Zeithaml., V., & Berry, L. (1988, Spring). SERVQUAL: A multiple-item scale for measuring consumer perceptions of service quality. *Journal of Retailing, 64,* 12-40.

Perdue, R. (1996). Target marketing selection and marketing strategy: The Colorado downhill skiing industry. *Journal of Travel Research, 34*(4), 39-46.

Peter, J. P., & Olson, J. C. (1990). *Consumer behavior and marketing strategy* (2nd ed.). Homewood, IL: Irwin.

Porter, M. E. (1980). *Competitive strategy: Techniques for analyzing industries and competitors.* New York: The Free Press.

Porter, M. E. (1991). Towards a dynamic theory of strategy. *Strategic Management Journal, 12,* 95-117.

Peter, J. P., & Donnelly, J. H. Jr. (1991). *A preface to marketing management* (5th ed). Homewood, IL: Irwin.

Powers, T. (1990). *Marketing hospitality.* New York: John Wiley & Sons.

Price, L. L., Arnould, E. J., & Tierney, P. (1995). Going to extremes: Managing service encounters and assessing provider performance. *Journal of Marketing, 59*(2), 83-97.

Purushottam, P., & Krishnamurthi, L. (1996). Measuring the dynamic effects of promotions on brand choice. *Journal of Marketing Research, 33,* 20-35.

Puto, C. P. (1987). The framing of buying decisions. *Journal of Consumer Research, 14,* 301-315.

Quelch, J. A., Dolan, R. J., & Kosnik, T. J. (1993). *Marketing Management: Text and cases.* Homewood, IL: Irwin.

Quinn, J. B. (1985). Managing innovation: Controlled chaos. *Harvard Business Review, 85*(3), 73-84.

Reich, A. Z. (1990). *The Restaurant Operator's Manual.* New York: Van Nostrand Reinhold.

Reich, A. Z. (1997a). Improving the effectiveness of destination positioning. *Tourism Analysis, 2*(1), 37-53.

Reich, A. Z. (1997b). *Marketing management for the hospitality industry: A strategic approach.* New York: John Wiley & Sons.

Reilly, M. D. (1990, Spring). Free elicitation of descriptive adjectives for tourism image assessment. *Journal of Travel Research,* 21-25.

Reilly, M. D., & Millikin, N. L. (1994). *Longitudinal stability of tourist images.* Travel & Tourism Research Association, 1-21.

Ries, A. (1988). The mind is the ultimate battlefield. *Journal of Business Strategy, 9*(4), 4-7.

Ries, A. (1992). The discipline of the narrow focus. *Journal of Business Strategy, 13*(6), 3-9.

Ring, L. J., Newton, D. A., Borden, N. H. Jr., & Farris, P. W. (1989). *Decisions in marketing* (2nd ed.). Homewood IL: BPI/Irwin.

Robertson, T. S., Eliashberg, J., & Rymon, T. (1995). New product announcement signals and incumbent reactions. *Journal ofMarketing, 59*(3), 1-15.

Robinson, J. (1948). *The economics of imperfect competition.* London: Macmillan.

Rokeach, M. (1960). *The open and closed mind: Investigations into the nature of belief sytems and personality systems.* New York: Basic Books.

Rokeach, M. (1968). *Beliefs, attitudes, and values.* San Francisco: Jossey-Bass. (5th printing, 1975).

Rokeach, M. (1973). *The nature of human values.* New York: Free Press.

Rosenberg, M. J. (1956). Cognitive structure and attitudinal affect. In M. J. Fishbein (Ed.), *Readings in attitude theory and management* (pp. 325-331). New York: John Wiley.

Ross, E. B. (1985). Making money with proactive pricing. *Harvard Business Review, 84*(6), 145-155.

Runkel, P. J., & McGrath, J. E. (1972). *Research on human behavior: A systematic guide to method.* New York: Holt, Rinehart, Winston.

Scott, J. E., & Lamont, L. M. (1973). Relating consumer values to consumer behavior: A model and method for investigation. In T. V. Greer (Ed.), *1973 combined proceedings: Increasing marketing productivity and conceptual and methodological foundations of marketing,* series No. 35 (pp. 283-288). Chicago: American Marketing Association.

Schiffman, L. G., & Kanuk, L. L. (1991). *Consumer behavior* (4th ed.). Englewood Cliffs, NJ: Prentice-Hall.

Schmitt, B. H., Simonson, A., & Marcus, J. (1995). Managing corporate image and identity. *Long Range Planning, 28*(5), 82-92.

Schnedler, D. E. (1996). Using strategic market models to predict customer behavior. *Sloan Management Review, 37*(3), 85-92.

Selin, S., & Chavez, D. (1995). Developing an evolutionary tourism partnership model. *Annals of Tourism Research, 22,* 844-856.

Shaw, M. (1992). Positioning and Price: Merging theory, strategy, and tactics. *Hospitality Research Journal, 15*(2), 31-39.

Sherif, C. W., Sherif, M., & Nevergall, R. E. (1965). *Attitude and attitude change: The social judgment-involvement approach.* Westport, CT: Greenwood Press.

Sheth, J. N., Newman, B. I., & Gross, B. L. (1991). *Consumption values and market choices.* Cincinnati, OH: South-Western.

Shostack, G. L. (1987). Service positioning through structural change. *Journal of Marketing, 51*(1), 34-43.

Simon, C. J., & Sullivan, M. W. (1990). *The measurement and determinants of brand equity: A financial approach.* Unpublished manuscript, University of Chicago, Graduate School of Business.

Simon, H. A. (1993). Strategy and organizational evolution. *Strategic Management Journal, 14,* 131-142.

Sirgy, M. J. (1997). *Presentation on promotional strategies.* Blacksburg, VA: Virginia Tech.

Smith, D. C., Andrews, J., & Blevins, T. R. (1992). The role of competitive analysis in implementing a market orientation. *Journal of Services Marketing, 6*(1), 23-36.

Snepenger, D., & Milner, L. (1990, *Spring*). Demographic and situational correlates of business travel. *Journal of Travel Research,* 27-32.

Snow, C. C., & Hrebiniak, L. G. (1980). Strategy, distinctive competence, and organizational performance. *Administrative Science Quarterly, 25,* 317-337.

Spiggle, S., & Sewall, A. S. (1987). A choice sets model of retail selection. *Journal of Marketing, 51,* 97-11.

Stalk, G. Evans, P., & Shulman, L. E. (1992). Competing on capabilities: The new rules of corporate strategy. *Harvard Business Review, 70*(2), 57-69.

Steenkamp, J. B., Trijp, H., & Ten Berge, J. (1994). Perceptual mapping based on idiosyncratic sets of attributes. *Journal of Marketing Research, 31*(1), 15-27.

Swinyard, W. R., & Struman, K. D. (1986). Market segmentation: Finding the heart of your restaurant's market. *The Cornell Hotel and Restaurant Administration Quarterly, 27*(1), 88-96.

Talley, W. (1968). Marketing research and development: Neglected way to profit growth. In R. L. Day (Ed.), *Concepts for modern marketing* (pp. 291-303). Scranton, PA: International Textbook.

Thomas, H., & Gardner, D. (Eds.). (1985). *Strategic marketing and management.* New York: John Wiley & Sons.

Thompson, A. A. Jr., & Strickland, A. U. III. (1993). *Strategic management.* Homewood, IL: Irwin.

Topfer, A. (1995). New products—cutting the time to market. *Long Range Planning, 28*(2), 61-78.

Tse, E. C. (1988). Defining corporate strengths and weaknesses: Is it essential for successful strategy implementation? *Hospitality Education and Research Journal, 12*(2), 57-63.

Tuan, Y. (1975). Images and mental maps. *Annals of the Association of American Geographers, 65,* 205-213.

Urban, G. L. & Star, S. H. (1991) *Advanced marketing strategy: Phenomena, analysis, and decisions.* Englewood Cliffs, NJ: Prentice-Hall.

Wicker, A. W. (1969). Attitudes vs. actions: The relationship of verbal and overt behavioral responses to attitude objects. *Journal of Social Issues, 25,* 41-78.

Wind, Y., & Robertson, T. S. (1983). Marketing strategy: New directions for theory and research. *Journal of Marketing, 47*(2), 12-25.

Wyer, R. S. Jr., & Srull, T. K. (1989). Person memory and judgment. *Psychological Review, 96*(1), 58-83.

Yuan, M. S., & Yuan, S. M. (1996). Sixteen versus nine expenditure categories in tourism surveys: Is there a difference? *Journal of Travel Research, 34*(4), 59-62.

■ Index